Number 131
Fall 2011

New Directions for Evaluation

Sandra Mathison
Editor-in-Chief

Really New Directions in Evaluation: Young Evaluators' Perspectives

Sandra Mathison
Editor

REALLY NEW DIRECTIONS IN EVALUATION: YOUNG EVALUATORS' PERSPECTIVES
Sandra Mathison (ed.)
New Directions for Evaluation, no. 131
Sandra Mathison, Editor-in-Chief

Microfilm copies of issues and articles are available in 16mm and 35mm, as well as microfiche in 105mm, through University Microfilms Inc., 300 North Zeeb Road, Ann Arbor, MI 48106-1346.

New Directions for Evaluation is indexed in Cambridge Scientific Abstracts (CSA/CIG), Contents Pages in Education (T & F), Higher Education Abstracts (Claremont Graduate University), Social Services Abstracts (CSA/CIG), Sociological Abstracts (CSA/CIG), and Worldwide Political Sciences Abstracts (CSA/CIG).

NEW DIRECTIONS FOR EVALUATION (ISSN 1097-6736, electronic ISSN 1534-875X) is part of The Jossey-Bass Education Series and is published quarterly by Wiley Subscription Services, Inc., A Wiley Company, at Jossey-Bass, 989 Market Street, San Francisco, CA 94103-1741.

SUBSCRIPTIONS cost $89 for U.S./Canada/Mexico; $113 international. For institutions, agencies, and libraries, $295 U.S.; $335 Canada/Mexico; $369 international. Prices subject to change.

EDITORIAL CORRESPONDENCE should be addressed to the Editor-in-Chief, Sandra Mathison, University of British Columbia, 2125 Main Mall, Vancouver, BC V6T 1Z4, Canada.

www.josseybass.com

Editorial Policy and Procedures

New Directions for Evaluation, a quarterly sourcebook, is an official publication of the American Evaluation Association. The journal publishes empirical, methodological, and theoretical works on all aspects of evaluation. A reflective approach to evaluation is an essential strand to be woven through every issue. The editors encourage issues that have one of three foci: (1) craft issues that present approaches, methods, or techniques that can be applied in evaluation practice, such as the use of templates, case studies, or survey research; (2) professional issues that present topics of import for the field of evaluation, such as utilization of evaluation or locus of evaluation capacity; (3) societal issues that draw out the implications of intellectual, social, or cultural developments for the field of evaluation, such as the women's movement, communitarianism, or multiculturalism. A wide range of substantive domains is appropriate for *New Directions for Evaluation;* however, the domains must be of interest to a large audience within the field of evaluation. We encourage a diversity of perspectives and experiences within each issue, as well as creative bridges between evaluation and other sectors of our collective lives.

The editors do not consider or publish unsolicited single manuscripts. Each issue of the journal is devoted to a single topic, with contributions solicited, organized, reviewed, and edited by a guest editor. Issues may take any of several forms, such as a series of related chapters, a debate, or a long article followed by brief critical commentaries. In all cases, the proposals must follow a specific format, which can be obtained from the editor-in-chief. These proposals are sent to members of the editorial board and to relevant substantive experts for peer review. The process may result in acceptance, a recommendation to revise and resubmit, or rejection. However, the editors are committed to working constructively with potential guest editors to help them develop acceptable proposals.

Sandra Mathison, Editor-in-Chief
University of British Columbia
2125 Main Mall
Vancouver, BC V6T 1Z4
CANADA
e-mail: nde@eval.org

Contents

EDITOR'S NOTES

This issue of *New Directions for Evaluation* (NDE) marks a milestone—the 25th anniversary of the American Evaluation Association (AEA). NDE is an official publication of AEA and has been a crucial means for the Association to foster and promote the professionalization of evaluation through thematic discussions of theory and practice in evaluation. NDE was first published in 1978 under the name *New Directions for Program Evaluation*, although the title became *New Directions for Evaluation* in 1995 in acknowledgement of the broader scope of evaluation. During the early years, NDE was affiliated with one of AEA's predecessor organizations, the Evaluation Research Society. Over the years, NDE has been stewarded by a number of editors-in-chief, including Scarvia Anderson, Ronald Wooldridge, Ernest House, Mark Lipsey, Nick Smith, Willam Shadish, Lois-ellin Datta, Jennifer Greene, Gary Henry, Jean King, and myself.

In the first issue of 1978, then editor-in-chief Scarvia Anderson wrote, "Program evaluation is not a new enterprise" (Anderson, 1978, vii). In her introduction, Anderson points to the development of evaluation as a "distinct field of activity." She falls short of characterizing evaluation as a discipline or profession, but acknowledges the meaningfulness of the creation of evaluation associations, publications, and the availability of government funding to investigate the success of the Great Society initiatives. There can be little doubt that in the years since NDE was launched evaluation has become a discipline, or, more accurately, a transdiscipline (Scriven, 1991) that permeates virtually every aspect of human endeavor. In every discipline, in every sector of society, in every institution, and in every organization evaluation is being conducted, sometimes by people who claim evaluation as their professional work and just as often by other professionals for whom evaluation is simply embedded in their work. AEA and NDE speak most directly to the former and face a future challenge of finding ways to speak to the latter.

Looking Back, Looking Ahead

Anniversaries are memorable moments, key elements of history. They are backward glances, ones that make us think about high and low points, but also provide glimpses into a future, ones that extend past successes, remedy shortcomings, and blaze new pathways. Taking the opportunity to pause at anniversaries is an opportunity for edification. In 2007, I edited an issue of NDE that looked back over the past 20 years of the journal to highlight important moments and enduring ideas in evaluation theory and practice (Mathison, 2007). That issue of NDE was devoted to what might be called

NEW DIRECTIONS FOR EVALUATION, no. 131, Fall 2011 © Wiley Periodicals, Inc., and the American Evaluation Association. Published online in Wiley Online Library (wileyonlinelibrary.com) • DOI: 10.1002/ev.370

the journal's "greatest hits"—those articles to which evaluators return time and again in their scholarship and evaluation practice. The chapters included in that retrospective were Egon G. Guba and Yvonna S. Lincoln's 1986 chapter, "But Is It Rigorous? Trustworthiness and Authenticity in Naturalistic Evaluation"; Mark Lipsey's 1993 chapter, "Theory as Method: Small Theories of Treatments"; Carol Weiss's 1997 "Theory-Based Evaluation: Past, Present, and Future"; and C. Bradley Cousins and Elizabeth Whitmore's 1998 "Framing Participatory Evaluation." These oft-referred-to chapters are about theoretical and conceptual ideas in evaluation, about foundational formulations that inform evaluators' practice. The 2007 NDE issue looks back at the ideas that have endured, the ideas that have captured the imagination of NDE readers.

The current issue of NDE, on the 25th anniversary of AEA, looks not back but ahead. Because NDE is a thematic, guest-edited journal, it tends to favor more mature, self-assured voices in evaluation. Guest editors are usually senior members of AEA and have been doing and thinking about evaluation for many years, even when they are writing about new directions in evaluation. The journal format does not lend itself easily to showcasing the voices of novice evaluators, those just entering the field and who will be the next generation of evaluation practitioners and theoreticians. As such, NDE has chosen on this anniversary to highlight those voices. In a call for proposals, young evaluators (those people in the field less than 5 years) were invited to share what matters to them, theoretically, conceptually, and practically, as they begin their professional lives as evaluators. From this call we received 139 proposals that were reviewed by the Editorial Board, and from which 20 were chosen for inclusion. The overwhelming response to the call for proposals is surely meaningful, although without further investigation one must speculate on that meaningfulness. It would seem at least that young evaluators want to talk about their evaluation practice, to explore the ideas they encounter in their education, and to contribute to the evolving transdiscipline of evaluation. This seems a positive sign for the future of the profession of evaluation.

What's on Young Evaluators' Minds?

The call for proposals was purposefully nonspecific and encouraged young evaluators to write about what matters most to them. The most frequent foci of the proposals were issues in evaluating particular evaluands (like youth programs, professional development, international programs, and so on); elaborations on or examples of using extant evaluation models (especially developmental evaluation, culturally responsive evaluation, evaluation capacity building, but others as well); and descriptions of good teaching and learning of evaluation. (See Figure 1.) Other topics included evaluation methods and techniques, evaluators' roles, evaluation use and the more contemporary

Figure 1. Foci of All Proposals in Response to the *NDE* Young Evaluators' Issue Call for Proposals

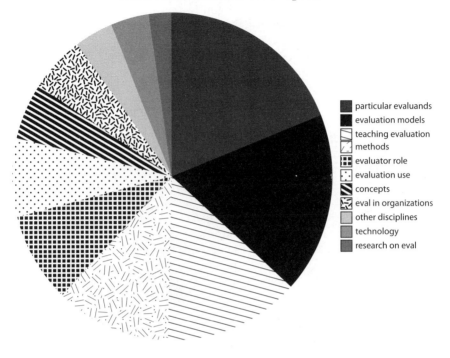

particular evaluands
evaluation models
teaching evaluation
methods
evaluator role
evaluation use
concepts
eval in organizations
other disciplines
technology
research on eval

notion of evaluation influence, conceptual ideas in evaluation (for example, validity, criteria), evaluation within organizational contexts (including internal evaluation), how evaluation can benefit from other disciplines, both the use of technology in evaluation and the evaluation of technology, and topics in research on evaluation. This describes the content of the proposals, but this analysis was not part of the selection of proposals for inclusion in this issue. Reviews by the *NDE* editorial board focused on a number of criteria, including clarity of the proposal, the "newness" of the topic, and its appeal to a broad audience of evaluators. As such, the proposals accepted and the chapters in this issue do not proportionally represent the topics in Figure 1. Figure 2 gives an overall impression of the topics covered in this *NDE* issue.

Many of the proposals submitted focused on issues and dilemmas in evaluating particular evaluands or provided examples of evaluations using extant evaluation models. These are surely worthy topics, and we respect the place these topics have in the minds of young evaluators, although we have not included these as chapters in this *NDE* issue. Instead we have selected chapters that reflect what may be glimpses into the future discourse in evaluation. Included are a number of chapters that build on what evaluation has

New Directions for Evaluation • DOI: 10.1002/ev

Figure 2. Foci of Chapters in the Young Evaluators' Perspectives Issue of *New Directions for Evaluation*

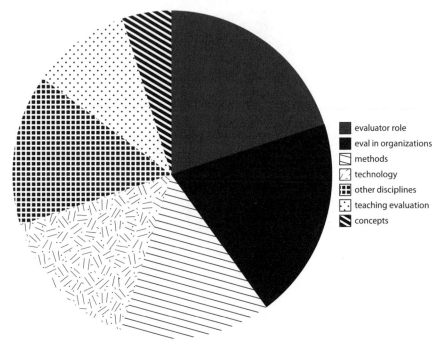

- ■ evaluator role
- ■ eval in organizations
- ◺ methods
- ▨ technology
- ⊞ other disciplines
- ⠋ teaching evaluation
- ◣ concepts

already learned from other disciplines by introducing us to new possibilities from political psychology, the humanities, sociocultural theory, and the notion of basic social science in the chapters by McBride, Smith, Perry, and Blagg. We are also challenged in the chapters by Coryn and Hobson, Evergreen, and Galloway to think about techniques or methods we use, both at a practical and conceptual level. Chapters by Bheda, Schlueter, Robinson, and White and Boulton raise questions about who evaluators are, how they interact with others, and the roles they assume in their practice. And chapters by Baxter, Derrick-Mills, Hoffman, and Jansen van Rensburg confront, in various ways, conundrums in thinking about and doing evaluation within organizations, either from an external or internal perspective. Price and Wilson deal with concepts that affect much evaluation—performance management and effectiveness engineering. And the last three chapters by Cohen, Galen and Grodzicki, and Nord focus on using technology in evaluation or challenges in evaluating technology.

Time will tell if the topics in this issue are foundational. For now, we celebrate AEA's 25th anniversary by shining a spotlight on what some of the next generation of evaluators is thinking about now.

NEW DIRECTIONS FOR EVALUATION • DOI: 10.1002/ev

References

Anderson, S. (1978). Editor's notes: The expanding role of program evaluation. *New Directions for Program Evaluation, 1*, vii–xii.

Mathison, S. (Ed.). (2007). *Enduring issues in evaluation: The 20th anniversary of the collaboration between NDE and AEA. New Directions for Evaluation, 114*.

Scriven, M. (1991). *Evaluation thesaurus* (4th ed.). Newbury Park, CA: Sage.

Sandra Mathison
Editor

SANDRA MATHISON *is a professor of education at the University of British Columbia, editor-in-chief of* New Directions for Evaluation, *and coeditor of* Critical Education.

McBride, D. F. (2011). Sociocultural theory: Providing more structure to culturally responsive evaluation. In S. Mathison (Ed.), *Really new directions in evaluation: Young evaluators'
perspectives. New Directions for Evaluation, 131*, 7–13.

1

Sociocultural Theory: Providing More Structure to Culturally Responsive Evaluation

Dominica F. McBride

Abstract

*Evaluation's "ancestors" have formed a strong foundation on which experienced,
nascent, and future evaluators can build. An area for growth and cultivation is
culturally responsive evaluation. The author describes sociocultural theory (ST),
a comprehensive theory explaining how culture influences human development,
and its potential for program evaluation. Although ST concretizes culture and
provides guidelines for culturally responsive research, it has never been applied
to program evaluation.* © Wiley Periodicals, Inc., and the American Evaluation Association.

ulture is the fabric of life, the theme that runs through humanity and
its expressions and behaviors. Culture encompasses, but is not limited to, the beliefs, values, norms, language, food, and clothing that
a group shares. It often guides behaviors, cognitions, decisions, institutions,
and governances. Because of this pervasiveness, the consideration and/or
study of culture is essential in program and policy development and evaluation. In development work, the study of culture can help identify what
problems exist, why they exist, and how to solve them. In evaluation, the
inclusion of culture is conducive to the full comprehension of the evaluand.

NEW DIRECTIONS FOR EVALUATION, no. 131, Fall 2011 © Wiley Periodicals, Inc., and the American Evaluation
Association. Published online in Wiley Online Library (wileyonlinelibrary.com) • DOI: 10.1002/ev.371

Thus, the field of program evaluation cannot ignore the undercurrent and force of culture and, with this recognition, has begun to emphasize and prioritize culture in its standards, principles, and work.

Culturally responsive evaluation (CRE) provides a set of guiding principles for evaluations (Frazier-Anderson, Hood, & Hopson, in press). In conducting CRE, the evaluator must manifest cultural competence (see Ridley, Mendoza, Kanitz, Angermeier, & Zenk, 1994) in every decision, action, tool, and step. The evaluation should be infused with and/or respond to the target group's cultural values, sensibilities, principles, feedback, and guidelines. If the evaluation or evaluator lacks this cultural responsiveness or sensitivity, then validity of the findings could be compromised (Kirkhart, 2010). Although a great guide for evaluators, some of the details of this framework and actualizing CRE in practice can be enhanced. This article describes how sociocultural theory (ST) can be applied to evaluation to bolster and supplement the current literature on CRE. It further provides examples of how this theory has been and could be used in both program development and evaluation.

The Russian psychologist Lev Vygotsky first developed sociocultural theory in the early 20th century, an era of confusion and political conflict (Rosa & Montero, 1990). During Vygotsky's professional life a debate existed between psychological theories focused on "heredity and environment" versus intangible ideals with an emphasis on consciousness. By integrating ideas from various disciplines and connecting the dichotomized materialism and consciousness, Vygotsky developed an inclusive theory focused on analysis on multiple levels (Rosa & Montero, 1990), culture, and human development (Rogoff, 2003). With a foundation of philosophical integration, ST holds that culture is seen as mutually constituted by individuals, society, biology, ecology, and history (Rogoff, 2003). Thus, it asserts the influence of one aspect of a situation cannot be seen as separate from another. Further, the true understanding of an individual is encompassed in the understanding of the contexts and history of that individual (Rogoff, 2003). Because of this imperative, a sociocultural approach has the potential to add comprehensiveness and cohesion as well as bolster human connectivity and compassion. Examining one's own cultural influences and potential biases, attempting to abate ethnocentrism, an openness and direct desire to learn about another's culture, history, and the dynamics that mold them, moving beyond a deficit-oriented mentality, "separating value judgments from explanations," and spending significant time with those that one is researching (or evaluating) and learning from them are all aspects of ST research (Rogoff, 2003). Openness, comprehensiveness, and unity are the core of ST, and these principles can lead to a more human way of seeing humans. The following sections present concrete ways to apply ST to bolster evaluations and cohesive human connections within evaluations.

Rogoff and Chavajay (1995) and Rogoff (2003) outline basic assumptions in sociocultural research (see Table 1.1). McBride (2009) conducted a study guided by ST, conceptualizing a culturally responsive family health

Table 1.1. Connecting Sociocultural Theory (ST) to Evaluation Practice

Assumption in ST	Explanation of Assumption	Examples from McBride (2009)
Unit of analysis is the sociocultural activity.	The activity must be examined with culture considered and in its natural environment.	Use of focus groups as a data-collection tool, not only attending to the content of the group but observing and notating the group process. Both the group *content* and *process* gave insight into the target culture. Although the naturally occurring activity of group process was tainted by external facilitation, the cultural dynamics were still apparent and notable.
Understanding of humanity requires study of both the development (individual, community, and species) and interpersonal and group processes of people.	Study local history and how that affects present living and how culture (including biology) influences the changes and development of a community over time.	Data focused on the contextual and cultural history of the target community. Data were collected from historic documents and studies, documentation from local leaders, and interviews with local leaders.
Human dynamics are affected by individual, interpersonal, and community dynamics, which are inseparable.	Individual, social, and cultural processes are not perceived and studied in isolation; while one aspect may be of particular focus in a given study, the influence of the other two facets is always considered.	Emphasis on the interpersonal and cultural–institutional aspects of families' lives and the interconnection of the individual, social, and cultural processes. Focus group and interview questions targeted each of the processes and inquired on how they could be included and/or addressed by a program.
Variation and similarity in a community are equally pertinent and considered simultaneously.	There is more variation within groups than between groups and includes methodology that highlights this fact and/or allows for these similarities and differences to be examined.	(a) Using a mixed methods design, (b) conducting re-search on the greater culture and history, (c) inquiring if themes applied to the local community, (d) allowing room for varied opinions and interpretations, and, finally, (e) avoiding automatically generalizing the study's find-ings to other communities, even of the same ethnicity.

(*Continued*)

Table 1.1. (Continued)

Assumption in ST	Explanation of Assumption	Examples from McBride (2009)
Research question drives the methods; the methods do not drive the question.	Use the method, be it psychological, ethnographic, and so on, or collection of methods best suited to answer the question and understand the relevant cultural and human dynamics.	Use of both qualitative and quantitative methods, from various social sciences. Given the goal of the study, community input and understanding was essential and led to using qualitative methods. Quantitative methods were included to ascertain the degree of cultural–historical congruence between the greater and local ethnic group and the variation within the local group.
Researchers must be self-reflective and aware of their own cultural influences and the institutions that affect them and their work.	Researchers recognize the influence of their own culture and institutions on their perspectives and scholarly work. This direction requires self-reflexivity beyond the conscious imperatives and into underlying assumptions.	Addressed by exploring their own cultural processes and assumptions and the various institutions within the larger academic institution that implicitly and explicitly influenced this research.

program for an African American community. The first step in the research process was to conduct a literature review on the larger African American community, ascertaining cultural–historical themes (i.e., religion/spirituality, extended family, and racial socialization). The applicability of these greater factors was assessed with the target Black community. The second step was to construct a community advisory board that advised on the actions and direction of the study as it related to the local community. Given the importance of history and context, eight interviews on local Black history and policy were completed with local community leaders. Relevant historical and current documentation was reviewed to supplement interviews. A total of 10 focus groups were conducted with parents/guardians ($N = 54$) and family health workers ($N = 17$) in the community, gaining their input on the structure and content of the program and how to integrate the cultural–historical factors. Finally, after data analysis, a final focus group was conducted with a sample of the previous focus group members to ascertain the validity of the findings.

As can be seen in Table 1.1, these assumptions are designed to engender a robust understanding of cultural processes through research. The first assumption focuses on the unit of analysis of the research, asserting culturally and naturally occurring activity should be of focus. Regarding program evaluation, the data-collection method of observation can be used and complemented with the ethnographic method of thick description (Geertz, 1973). The thick description should elucidate the activity, all of those involved, and the context. The evaluator should attempt to include these methods in the assessment of the community prior to the implementation of the evaluation and in the evaluation itself.

The focus of the second assumption is on change. Program evaluators can recognize that an evaluand may be different over time. The program and stakeholders assessed at one time may look different at another, with the change of context and people. One way an evaluator could apply this assumption is with the study of history and context prior to and during the implementation of an evaluation.

The third assumption highlights the complexity of human beings as it relates to internal and external factors that affect thinking and behavior. It places particular focus on the individual, interpersonal, and contextual dynamics of a given situation. In evaluation, the evaluator can consider each variable in assessing the various aspects of the program and employ methods that examine the impact of each on a program and people. This can also include the analysis of how program activities lie at the intersection of individual, social, and cultural processes and how each influences the effectiveness of a program.

In the process of bolstering cultural competence, we can sometimes make the mistake of creating and perpetuating stereotypes (e.g., in working with Latinos, an evaluator should assess machismo). The fourth assumption goes against this tendency, recognizing both the similarities and variation within and between communities. Evaluators can apply this notion in their perspective and methodology by using a diversity of methods (e.g., focus groups, observation, surveys) to see both the commonalities and differences within and between communities. They can also be conscious of the tendency to generalize a cultural norm to an entire group while also seeing the similarities between their own cultural norms and others.

Like the field of program evaluation, ST is both inter- and transdisciplinary. ST holds that in order to gain a complete understanding of culture (e.g., the psychological, biological, ecological, and historical aspects) through research, the research methods and design need to be informed by various disciplines. In order to accomplish this, evaluators could gain additional training in various data collection methods/designs or create multidisciplinary teams.

To understand others' cultural norms, one must study and know one's own, and thus, there is a need for a multifaceted cultural self-exploration for researchers (Rogoff, 2003; Rogoff & Chavajay, 1995). Evaluators can apply this by assessing not only themselves as cultural beings and their own varying contexts, but also the institutions in their work lives and in the field of program evaluation. Future evaluation research could answer questions such as: What are the tacit institutions in the field of program evaluation? How do these institutions manifest in power relations between evaluators and evaluands? How do they display themselves in evaluation designs?

Given these six assumptions and their consideration of culture, human development, and human dynamics, ST proves to be a viable and apt framework to supplement CRE and further inform evaluations. This approach can add to the robustness and validity of an evaluation. Not only does it help with structure, but it also can bolster the compassion and connectedness evaluators should have with stakeholders. The respect for others that ST encourages renders relationships that can both enhance the evaluation and be ancillary to stakeholders in the process, especially when evaluators are often viewed as threatening. Overall, with the strong foundation of evaluation, ST can help to build and, in the process, hone an evaluation through enhanced understanding and connection.

References

Frazier-Anderson, P., Hood, S., & Hopson, R. (in press). An African American culturally responsive evaluation system. In S. Lapan, M. Quartaroli, & F. Riemer (Eds.), *Qualitative research: An introduction to methods and designs.* San Francisco, CA: Jossey-Bass.

Geertz, C. (1973). *The interpretation of cultures: Selected essays.* New York, NY: Basic Books.

Kirkhart, K. E. (2010). Eyes on the prize: Multicultural validity and evaluation theory. *American Journal of Evaluation, 31,* 400–413.

McBride, D. F. (2009). *Moving towards holistic equity: A process of developing a culturally responsive family health program* (Doctoral dissertation). Retrieved from Dissertations & Theses: Full Text. (Publication No. AAT 3391851)

Ridley, C. R., Mendoza, D. W., Kanitz, B. E., Angermeier, L., & Zenk, R. (1994). Cultural sensitivity in multicultural counseling: A perceptual schema model. *Journal of Counseling Psychology, 41*, 125–136.

Rogoff, B. (2003). *The cultural nature of human development.* New York, NY: Oxford University Press.

Rogoff, B., & Chavajay, P. (1995). What's become of research on the cultural basis of cognitive development. *American Psychologist, 50*, 859–877.

Rosa, A., & Montero, I. (1990). The historical context of Vygotsky's work: A sociohistorical approach. In L. C. Moll (Ed.), *Vygotsky and education: Instructional implications and applications of sociohistorical psychology* (pp. 59–88). New York, NY: Cambridge University Press.

DOMINICA F. MCBRIDE *is co-founder/co-president of The HELP Institute, Inc., and head of the research division of the Community Mental Health Council, Inc.*

NEW DIRECTIONS FOR EVALUATION • DOI: 10.1002/ev

Smith, D. A. (2011). Making the case for the humanities in evaluation training. In S. Mathison (Ed.), *Really new directions in evaluation: Young evaluators' perspectives. New Directions for Evaluation, 131,* 15–20.

2

Making the Case for the Humanities in Evaluation Training

Deborah A. Smith

Abstract

The author argues that evaluators who are comfortable with the interpretation of competing values—an ability that can be fostered by exposure to the humanities— might be able to contribute significant advances toward finding a better balance of methodologies in an ever-more-ambiguous world. This argument is made by describing a humanities-informed evaluation graduate course. Black-and-white worldviews and one-size-fits-all solutions are hard to reconcile in evaluation environments increasingly characterized by multiculturalism, complexity, and uncertainty. The author reflects on the place of value judgments in the graduate education of future evaluators, not as something to avoid, but as an opportunity to improve needed skills. © Wiley Periodicals, Inc., and the American Evaluation Association.

A Google search on *evaluation syllabus* yields an enticing range of evaluation courses at the graduate level. The commonalities in most are fundamental competencies in statistics, analysis, research design, and quantitative and qualitative methods that any master of arts or doctoral candidate who wants to work in evaluation should master. Few lessons in these syllabi deal with the issue of value judgments. The evaluator-as-judge is not a role that instructors advise students to assert, except in cases of unusual circumstances or last resort (Rossi, Freeman, & Lipsey, 1999, p. 269). Instead, evaluators-in-training are encouraged to produce findings and discuss the results' implications; they are adjured not to mistake interpretations for judgments (Patton, 2002, p. 331).

Like it or not, though, evaluation is about variations of value and scaling. As Michael Scriven put it 20 years ago, "Evaluation is the process of determining the merit, worth, and value of things, and evaluations are the products of that process" (Scriven, 1991, p. 1). As evaluation environments become increasingly characterized by multiculturalism, complexity, and uncertainty, the potential for perplexity on the part of evaluators also rises. In the words of Jonah Lehrer, "Just because an idea is true doesn't mean it can be proved. And just because an idea can be proved doesn't mean it's true. When the experiments are done, we still have to choose what to believe" (Lehrer, 2010, p. 57). What might the future of evaluation look like if the next generation of graduate education deliberately sought to help resolve the quandaries for young evaluators through a more diversified curriculum, where both choice and proof are not only valued, but intelligently implemented?

A Humanities-Informed Evaluation Course

What follows are some reflections on an evaluation "fantasy" class whose purpose is to teach the fine balance between science and art in the task of making judgments.

Goals and Objectives

The course objectives derive from Scriven's ideas about the differences between evaluation and social science research (Coffman, 2003/2004, p. 7). Scriven reminds us that evaluators not only need the facility to test hypotheses, but three other important skills as well: the abilities to search for side effects, deal with controversy, and synthesize information. Clearly, the skills that Scriven requires of evaluators are central to all critical thinking, not just humanities scholarship. Still, because the humanities disciplines embrace human values in all their messy disarray, they therefore provide useful resources for developing these skills.

Table 2.1 illustrates the links among each skill/objective to a more abstract goal/theme of what it means to be human, and then to some possible teaching metaphors or analogies—the tools of the humanist.

Linking Evaluation Skills and Humanities Themes

Nothing in Life Is Certain: Skills = Searching for Side Effects

As anyone who has tried to create the perfect logic model knows, the ideal and the real are often far apart. Things may get off to a good start but can quickly head in the wrong direction because of unanticipated events or

Table 2.1. Connecting Evaluator Skills With Humanities Themes and Teaching Foci

Scriven's Skills: Course Objectives	Humanities Themes: Course Goals	Teaching Metaphors and Analogies
Evaluators need the ability to search for side effects	Nothing in human life is certain; fostering functional flexibility with the unexpected results that wait to be discovered in evaluation	Hidden in plain view Detours on the road Murphy's Law Plus ça change c'est plus la même chose The Butterfly Effect The Serenity Prayer
Evaluators need the ability to deal with controversy	The common denominator of humanity is its diversity; fostering appreciation for controversies in evaluation that reflect many perspectives	Prisms Chameleons Selective amnesia False dichotomies Double consciousness Winners write the history books Pyrrhic victory Reconciliation
Evaluators need the ability to synthesize information	Human creativity, including knowledge creation, demands choices; exploring synthesis as a value-laden part of evaluation	Hobson's choice Horns of a dilemma Forks in the road The road never taken Creative destruction Knowledge is power Sum of the parts

unforeseen consequences. Think of the detours as unpredictable but omnipresent side effects waiting to be discovered. One goal of this class segment is to help students learn to be functionally flexible. What is Plan B, all the way to Plan Z? Are any parts of the intervening plans salvageable? Or does the attempt to hang onto what isn't working only leave one stuck in the labyrinth? Was the source of the derailment something that at first appeared as inconsequential as the flap of a butterfly's wings? Are there clues to finding a way forward right under your nose? A second goal is akin to the gambler's advice: when coping with Murphy's Law, "know when to hold 'em, fold 'em, walk away, or run" (Schlitz, 1978).

Diversity Is the Universal Constant: Skills = Dealing With Controversy

The beauty of humanity is in our differences, but at the same time differences can cause ugly controversies. Evaluators never work in isolation with the luxury that theirs are the only values that matter. The list of possible stakeholders might include administrators, board members, courts, the X-generation, young fathers, and zealots of all stripes. It is very hard for beginning evaluators to remember—one goal of this class segment—that all of these stakeholders view the program and evaluation from different perspectives. Stakeholders may not even see the same things, and they may not appreciate the role of the outside evaluator, who might see false dichotomies where insiders perceive conflicts. However, recognizing that other viewpoints exist is only half of this skill set. A second goal is learning to reconcile the differences.

Values Underlie Every Choice: Skills = Synthesizing Information

The goal of the synthesis segment of the class is to help students understand that the assemblage of new knowledge from disparate parts invariably requires choices, minimally, in how the evaluator chooses to interpret the data. Part of that process is learning to recognize (a) the biases of the data and of the evaluator, (b) the benefits of a learning community in creating knowledge versus the dangers of groupthink, and (c) the ever-present possibility that in building knowledge from many parts, the new sum may not necessarily add up to more. A second goal is to help students recognize that when some modes of inquiry are privileged above all other forms of knowledge, the unhelpful result (as well as unrealistic, perhaps unethical, and probably inaccurate) is to foster foregone conclusions. The purpose of synthesis, therefore, is not to replace or obscure what came before but to integrate and balance.

Texts and Curriculum Materials

The course's three suggested core texts successfully support the search for middle ground between science and art in evaluation. *Rational Choice in an Uncertain World: The Psychology of Judgment and Decision Making* (Hastie & Dawes, 2010) is an excellent introduction to the evaluator's tasks of "rating and ranking." *How Professors Think: Inside the Curious World of Academic Judgment* (Lamont, 2010) explores the different ways that social scientists and humanists go about their work as evaluators in a specific context, that is, the determination of academic fellowships and research grants. This book is also a good overview of what the novice evaluator educated in one discipline might encounter when collaborating with colleagues from other disciplines. *Policy Paradox: The Art of Political Decision Making* (Stone, 2001) examines the trade-offs that characterize decisions by public figures, and often lead them to call in an evaluator. Stone's book points out how "politics" are at play in all human interactions; her thoughtful, yet disquieting, analysis of the process by which we make choices is transferable to any evaluation setting. These core texts are meant to ground the course in a neutral space that gives equal weight to the methodologies and perspectives of all academic disciplines.

Beyond the core texts, however, instructors will have their own favorite resources that remind them of Scriven's skills for evaluators, and students

Table 2.2. Humanities-Based Resources Connecting to Course Themes and Goals

Scriven's Skills/Course Themes and Objectives	Author/Title/Date/Format of Possible Teaching Resources
Searching for side effects: Dealing with the unexpected is the norm, actions may have unintended results, solutions may be at hand all along if you know where to look.	Woody Allen, *The Kugelmass Episode* (1977 short story) Leonard Bernstein, *Candide* (1956 operetta based on Voltaire's 1759 satire, 2005 Great Performances DVD) Joseph Heller, *Catch 22* (1961 novel, 1970 film) Edgar Allan Poe, *The Purloined Letter* (1844 short story) Monty Python, *Nobody Expects the Spanish Inquisition* (1970 comedy sketch) Kevin Willmott, *C.S.A.: The Confederate States of America* (2004 mockumentary)
Dealing with controversy: Diversity is present not only between groups but within every individual; diversity applies to nonvisible differences, too.	W.E.B. Du Bois, *The Souls of Black Folk* (1903 nonfiction) Todd Haynes, *I'm Not There* (2007 film) Akira Kurosawa, *Rashomon* (1951 film) Charlotte Gilman Perkins, *The Yellow Wallpaper* (1892 short story) Oliver Sacks, *The Man Who Mistook His Wife for a Hat* (1985 nonfiction)
Synthesizing information: Sophisticated data need interpretation to be useful; how we know something influences what we understand about it.	Sebastian Junger, *The Perfect Storm* (1997 nonfiction, 2000 film) Charles Mackay, *Extraordinary Popular Delusions and the Madness of Crowds* (1841 nonfiction) Harold Ramis, *Groundhog Day* (1993 film) Fred Schepisi, *I.Q.* (1994 film) William Styron Jr., *Sophie's Choice* (1979 novel, 1982 film)

should be able to contribute material as well. For example, what if professors who use case studies about real programs, people, and places asked the class to spend 5 minutes talking about the values embodied in the case? Then, for the next session, they asked students to find poems that express those values, read them to the class, and explain the connection? In such an exercise, there is no right or wrong answer; the point of the lesson lies in the power of the humanities to inspire.

Table 2.2 is thus offered as only one list of possibilities where the book, film, or music suggests analogies and metaphors that connect to the course themes/goals. Although each title is listed for only one of Scriven's skill areas, they often overlap. That the humanities make us choose between multiple interpretations, and perhaps draw more than one conclusion, are central premises of the course.

Conclusions

Like the fantasy sports league, the humanities-based course outlined here is one that has never been tried—or evaluated—in an actual classroom. Whether learning outcomes would reflect the teaching objectives can only be imagined, too. That said, because both the rational and emotional sides of the brain are active in human decisions, surely it makes sense that evaluation educators should strive in their teaching to engage the whole. At minimum, an appreciation for humanities perspectives would give evaluators more tools to work with. At best, ensuring that human values are the heart of evaluation education could potentially contribute significant advances toward finding a better balance of methodologies in an ever-more-ambiguous world.

References

Coffman, J. (Winter 2003/2004). Michael Scriven on the differences between evaluation and social science research. *The Evaluation Exchange, 9*(4). Retrieved from http://www.hfrp.org/evaluation/the-evaluation-exchange/issue-archive/

Hastie, R. K., & Dawes, R. M. (2010). *Rational choice in an uncertain world: The psychology of judgment and decision making* (2nd ed.). Thousand Oaks, CA: Sage.

Lamont, M. (2010). *How professors think: Inside the curious world of academic judgment.* Cambridge, MA: Harvard University Press.

Lehrer, J. (2010, December 13). The truth wears off. *The New Yorker,* pp. 52–57.

Patton, M. (2002). *Qualitative research & evaluation methods* (3rd ed.). Thousand Oaks, CA: Sage.

Rossi, P., Freeman, H., & Lipsey, M. (1999). *Evaluation: A systematic approach* (6th ed.). Thousand Oaks, CA: Sage.

Schlitz, D. (1978). The gambler [Recorded by Kenny Rogers]. Century City, CA: United Artists.

Scriven, M. (1991). *Evaluation thesaurus* (4th ed.). Newbury Park, CA: Sage.

Stone, D. (2001). *Policy paradox: The art of political decision making* (2nd ed.). New York, NY: W. W. Norton & Co.

DEBORAH A. SMITH *is the grants and contracts specialist for the College of Humanities and Social Sciences, and lecturer in the MA Program in Public Administration, at Kennesaw State University in Georgia.*

NEW DIRECTIONS FOR EVALUATION • DOI: 10.1002/ev

Perry, S. M. (2011). Political psychology in evaluation: A theoretical framework. In S. Mathison (Ed.), *Really new directions in evaluation: Young evaluators' perspectives. New Directions for Evaluation, 131,* 21–26.

3

Political Psychology in Evaluation: A Theoretical Framework

S. Marshall Perry

Abstract

The author describes how political psychology, an emerging field that explores the intersection of political science and psychology, can help in conducting evaluations. For example, an evaluator might examine the validity of behavioral assumptions of programs, policies, or organizational mechanisms and people's motivations and subjective experiences within these contexts. An evaluator might also explore the normative orientations of programs and policies, for example, how target goals and implementers are politically framed in a positive or negative light. The author describes a framework for political psychology as applied to evaluation, a brief review of relevant literature and discussion of methodology, and an example of an evaluation informed by political psychology. © Wiley Periodicals, Inc., and the American Evaluation Association.

Political psychology has the potential to illuminate complexities when evaluators are concerned with why people or organizations behave in certain ways or how people subjectively experience a policy, community, or organizational practice. As the name implies, it explores the intersection of political science and psychology. This means that one examines relationships between individual internal processes such as thoughts, feelings, or motivations, and external actions such as political behavior, mechanisms, or norms. "Political behavior" is not limited to formal legislation, voting behavior, or international relations; it can include an explicit policy or implicit norm within an organization or group and the behavior of individuals within those normative assumptions. Political mechanisms can include a policy or standardized practice intended to guide human behavior, typically through symbolism, inducements, or sanctions. For example, if one were to evaluate an organization's goal of improved participation from its local community, the evaluator could employ a political psychology framework to explore the validity of behavioral assumptions inherent in different outreach mechanisms by examining the subjective experiences of various community members. Or, the evaluator could explore how the organization created the policy by examining the motivations and subjective feelings of different actors. Such an evaluation can occur within a context of political norms, which are determinations of what is good or right. It is grounded in a conceptualization of thought (and therefore, behavior) as a social endeavor as opposed to thought as autonomous and independently rational.

The belief that a person's view of him- or herself is shaped by others has a history in both psychological and political thought. Kant (1805) argued for the social nature of thinking in his *Critique of Pure Reason*, arguing that the mind reasons through organized social experience. Based upon experiences, the mind infers. Mead (1934) continued this stream of thought, asserting, "The individual experiences himself . . . not directly, but only indirectly, from the particular standpoints of other individual members of the same social group, or from the generalized standpoint of the social group as a whole to which he belongs" (1934, pp. 138–139).

Moscovici (1998) and others noted the social origin of perceptions and beliefs in conjunction with the human tendency to perceive and explain things with the use of representations and concepts. When someone reasons, ideas and beliefs are induced within the interconnected framework of his or her social world, as this world has provided cultural tools and cues. In other words, no knowledge or way of thinking is discrete; instead, it is connected with other ideas or beliefs within a person's self-concept. For example, Markus, Mullally, and Kitayama (1997) consider thinking in light of "selfways"—a community's normative ideas about being a person and the social practices, situations, and restrictions of everyday life that represent and foster these ideas. Organizational practices or policies come into vogue within the context of these selfways. This is not to say that individuals within a group cannot differ from one another, because the specifics of one's world will differ from others', and the way in which meanings might be organized or utilized will differ. Even as we experience our world externally, through the eyes of others, individual construals allow for different areas of focus and different meaning making.

Consideration of community and individual beliefs in light of practices or policies might sound similar to theory of action (Argyris & Schön, 1978). Theory of action creates a bridge between one's thoughts and one's actions.

Espoused theories include what someone explicitly knows about him- or herself, while theories-in-use are theories that are implied by one's behavior. Individuals engage in action strategies to manage their surroundings with an eye to consequences for themselves and for others. Governing values define an acceptable range of action strategies undertaken. In attempting to make theories of action explicit, an evaluator considers a person's mental map; this accounts for a person's values, beliefs, and motivations in understanding why certain behavior or action occurs that might seem in conflict with one's espoused theories.

> In this conundrum of dissonance between stated belief and actual practice lies a golden opportunity for reality testing: the heart of evaluation . . . In short, the user-focused approach challenges decision makers, program staff, funders, and other users to engage in reality testing, that is to test whether what they believe to be true (their espoused theory of action) is what actually occurs (theory-in-use). (Patton, 2008, p. 339)

A theory of action translates into a rational approach to policy analysis and program evaluation, albeit with strengths and weaknesses.

> . . . the concept can help analysts and actors articulate and appraise the relationship between a program's aims, activities, and outcomes . . . a "theories of action" perspective focuses on the premises of a policy in order to gauge the substantive viability of that policy. While potentially instructive, a "theories of action" analysis is limited because the substantive promise of policy is only one of many factors shaping the selection an implementation of education reforms. (Malen, Croninger, Muncey, & Jones, 2002, p. 114)

A political psychology approach builds upon theories of action by contextualizing thoughts and behaviors within political and/or institutional norms. This can translate to the recognition of viable alternatives within a political/institutional context when considering whether or not a course of action is an appropriate one.

How does this framework for political psychology potentially fit into the work of the evaluator? A starting point might come from anthropologist Clifford Geertz (1974), who emphasized the need to "see things from the native's point of view," but made it clear that attempting to understand an "other" from his or her own perspective is a tall order. Your disposition affects what you choose to examine and what you notice. Your biases shape your interpretations of what you have seen. While undergoing a process of meaning making, an evaluator's discovered truths are therefore tempered by his or her acknowledgement of his or her cultural situatedness.

Steele and Sherman (1999) attempt to meet Geertz's charge with their concept of an "afforded psychology." Emphasizing how the life-space of a young woman on welfare might differ from someone who is middle-class within the same culture, the framework notes that what seems problematic in one social stratum could be useful or even necessary in another. It therefore charges evaluators to consider how context "contributes to the content, organization, and functioning of one's psychological life" (Steele & Sherman, 1999, p. 394).

Evaluators are therefore charged with considering methodologies, assumptions, and ideologies before attempting to learn anything from some different other. The afforded psychology of an evaluator recognizes that when different groups are studied from one perspective, and when it is assumed that perspective is the universal one, misunderstandings can result and injustices may be committed. Hence, evaluators attempt to place themselves within another's "life-space" contexts as much as possible. Research that does not attempt to consider both the context of the researcher and subject is therefore suspect. That which is "truth" is situated within specific contexts. Because quantitative designs are built around the researcher's hypotheses, qualitative or mixed-methods research is of greater value for an evaluator using a political psychology framework. Experimental designs, while considered rigorous by traditional perspectives (e.g., Campbell & Stanley, 1963), are not appropriate for this mode of inquiry.

Evaluations that are concerned with why people behave or think a certain way, why a practice or policy came to be formalized, or how people experience certain policies or organizational practices are examples of when political psychology may be a useful framework for the evaluation.

Illustrating a Political Psychology Framework for Evaluation

In evaluating a middle school's ability-grouping mechanism, the school was considered successful by macrolevel indicators. However, Black and Latino students were still performing far below Asian American and White students, who disproportionately populated the high-ability group. I wanted to understand why this school, in a progressive community, maintained ability grouping, and I wanted to see how students experienced ability grouping. As someone who benefited from the "upper track" curriculum but felt disconnected from other Black students in my middle and high school, I expected there to be stark differences in how students felt about school and themselves as students.

I examined the self-concept of a diverse group of middle school students in three different settings: a low-ability, a high-ability, and a mixed classroom. For students that started in a mixed classroom, I followed them into the subsequent academic year to observe the transition into ability grouping. The mixed-methods evaluation included student questionnaires, classroom observations, and interviews with students, teachers, and administrators.

I found that for low-ability–group students, ability grouping can have effects upon students' identification with school, educational goals, and ability to receive positive or negative feedback. Students did not feel worse about themselves as students, but realigned their aspirations and definitions of what it means to be a good student. The high-performing students within ability-grouped classrooms were not immune to effects upon self-concept either. Some students grew to view their racial identity as oppositional to their academic self-concept; others felt less self-confident about their abilities.

Based on a political psychology framework, one might examine the relationship between self-concept and ability grouping as a mutually reinforcing one, therefore contextualizing students' self-concepts within classroom norms. Although many studies of ability grouping and tracking contrast high and low groups, I decided to follow a group of students from a mixed setting (in sixth grade) to a grouped one (in seventh) across two academic years. Interviews consisted predominantly of open-ended probes, such as "describe yourself," in an effort to understand the students' experiences and perspectives.

Pursuing my study with this political psychology framework led to some surprises. For some students, school was less a central part of their self-concept; these students changed little in moving from a mixed- to an ability-group setting. Teachers in the mixed setting did not treat all students equally, so I could not say that the cause of unequal outcomes was ability grouping. I also found that school leaders and teachers responded to the pressure of high-status parents and the inertia of existing teaching methods and values to water down policies promoting heterogeneous grouping.

Using political psychology as a framework for study design and analysis has been invaluable to me as an evaluator. As a theoretical framework, I believe it has the potential to illuminate complexities when evaluators are concerned with why people or organizations behave in certain ways or how people subjectively experience a policy, community, or organizational practice.

References

Argyris, C., & Schön, D. (1978). *Organizational learning: A theory of action perspective.* Reading, MA: Addison-Wesley.

Campbell, D., & Stanley, J. (1963). *Experimental and quasi-experimental designs for research.* Chicago, IL: Rand McNally.

Geertz, C. (1974). From the native's point of view: On the nature of anthropological understanding. *Bulletin of the American Academy of Arts and Sciences, 28*(1), 26–45.

Kant, I. (1805/1998). *Critique of pure reason.* New York, NY: Cambridge University Press.

Malen, B., Croninger, R., Muncey, D., & Jones, D. (2002). Reconstituting schools: Testing the theory of action. *Education Evaluation and Policy Analysis, 24*(2), 113–132.

Markus, H. R., Mullally, P., & Kitayama, S. (1997). Selfways: Diversity in modes of cultural participation. In U. Neisser & D. Jopling (Eds.), *The conceptual self in context: Culture, experience, self-understanding* (pp. 13–61). Cambridge, UK: Cambridge University Press.

Mead, G. (1934). *Mind, self, and society.* Chicago, IL: University of Chicago Press.

Moscovici, S. (1998). The history and actuality of social representations. In E. Flick (Ed.), *The psychology of the social* (pp. 209–247). New York: Cambridge University Press.

Patton, M. (2008.) *Utilization-focused evaluation.* Thousand Oaks, CA: Sage.

Steele, C., & Sherman, D. (1999). The psychological predicament of women on welfare. In D. Prentice & D. Miller (Eds.), *Cultural divides: Understanding and overcoming group conflict* (pp. 393–428). New York, NY: Russell Sage Foundation.

S. MARSHALL PERRY is an assistant professor at Dowling College in Long Island, NY.

Blagg, R. D. (2011). A bridge between basic social science and evaluation. In S. Mathison (Ed.), *Really new directions in evaluation: Young evaluators' perspectives. New Directions for Evaluation, 131*, 27–30.

4

A Bridge Between Basic Social Science and Evaluation

Robert D. Blagg

Abstract

The author argues that evaluators must forge a strong bridge between basic social science and evaluation. Realizing this potential will involve holding evaluation to a high standard, through advancing cutting-edge empirical methods, balancing demands for accountability, and providing direction for basic social science. Approaches such as theory-based evaluation and natural-variation research designs can demonstrate the importance of evaluation, and help evaluators to ensure that traffic of ideas between basic social science and evaluation runs efficiently in both directions. © Wiley Periodicals, Inc., and the American Evaluation Association.

New evaluators must rise to meet opportunities to forge a stronger bridge between basic social science and evaluation, provided by a movement in social science toward greater relevance and responsiveness to current social issues (Sayer, 2010). Strengthening the bridge means filling many of the empty holes left by debates of basic versus applied social science (e.g., Rossi, 1987). Continuing this construction project involves holding evaluation to a high standard, through advancing cutting-edge empirical methods, balancing demands for accountability, and providing direction for basic social science. Although fraught with pitfalls and challenges (e.g., political and practical), forging a bridge between basic and applied research provides evaluation with the opportunity to fulfill its potential as a catalyst for social science progress.

The Relationship Between Theory and Practice

Progress toward building this bridge is most recently evident in the advancement of theory-based evaluation (e.g., Chen & Rossi, 1983). As Scriven (1991) described it, evaluation involves empirical investigation utilizing techniques derived from the social sciences, and integrates conclusions with values or standards for what is being evaluated. The growth of theory-driven evaluation has shown that an approach to theory building is another aspect of basic social science, beside measurement and statistical approaches, that evaluators have found useful. Although the exact definition of theory in evaluation is debated, it is evident that program theories offer a logical framework for program evaluations (Chen, 2003; Weiss, 1997). Program theories not only offer structure for measurement and data collection, but provide a basis for expectation and explanation of program processes, outcomes, and their connections (e.g., Donaldson, 2005). The use of theory to drive evaluations also represents the application of a standard to which basic social science is held, and is contributing to the maturity of evaluation as a discipline. Further, theory building in evaluation may allow for more productive communication with basic social science regarding evaluation results, thereby strengthening the bridge and increasing its use. However, for evaluation to reach its potential as a social science hub, advances in theory must be coupled with advances in applied methods.

Rethinking the Meaning of Rigorous Design

This role as a focal point for social science also necessitates pushing the limits and standards of rigorous applied research methods, as the consequences of evaluation are often more immediate, relative to basic research. As Rossi (1987) suggested, what is typically at stake in a basic social science journal article is the reputation of the author, but a poorly conceived or conducted evaluation may alter a policy or affect the course of a program and its stakeholders. Newer approaches (e.g., cluster, multisite, rapid assessment) to evaluation of multifaceted programs exemplify such advances.

For complex or multisite programs random assignment is practically or politically prohibitive; thus, establishing internal validity is often a challenge. But an approach to multisite evaluation that views the natural variation of a program and its environment as having explanatory power can provide support for causal connections. The natural variation approach takes advantage of inconsistent implementation, focusing on the differences within and across many program sites by capturing sources of naturally occurring variation so as to identify links with program outcomes and effects. This design and complementary data collection methods (e.g., mixed methods) are built to account for and explain the complexity of programs, rather than to control for it. This approach can provide evidence that programs implemented with less fidelity have little or no impact, whereas better-quality or more extensive implementations of a program yield more positive or fewer negative results. A recent practical example of this approach, The National Cross-Site Evaluation of High Risk Youth Programs, identified characteristics associated with strong substance-abuse prevention outcomes in 48 prevention programs (Springer et al., 2002). As was evident in this study, variation is the central facet of this design approach; thus comprehensively measuring relevant sources of variation is vital.

To capture variation across sites accurately, measurement must be developed based on what the site-level data collector observes. Specifically, a site observer must be able to capture unanticipated program processes or outcomes that may have unknown or unanticipated associations with program effects. Proper measurement includes data collection from multiple sources, including semistructured interviews and focus groups, observation, self-report measures, and archival data. Such diversity of site-level information may be captured through a site visit protocol including ranked, scaled, and open-ended items, which may be developed based upon a program theory (Springer et al., 2002). This approach to site-level data collection is imperative to the natural variation approach, as it aggregates large quantities of information from diverse sources (i.e., qualitative and quantitative). These aggregated data can be used to develop constructs (e.g., program context, implementation, outcomes, and effects) that represent the naturally occurring variation within and across sites. Thus, the natural-variation design and a comprehensive mixed-method measurement approach can support internal validity by identifying connections between program processes and effects, which may have more immediate implications for programs, stakeholders, and policy makers. However, examination of variation among program processes and effects across multiple sites can also provide support for external validity. Such rigorous applied studies can and should inform the work of basic social science researchers, influencing the social relevance of their research programs, and alerting them to the dangers of overaggregation.

The Political Significance of Bridging Social Science and Evaluation

Conceptually the advantages of fortifying a bridge between basic social science and evaluation for theory building and methodological advancement may seem obvious, but practically, as evaluators begin their professional lives, they quickly encounter increased politicization of evaluation, as the demand for accountability has put great emphasis on data-driven decision making. Such demands can serve as roadblocks to knowledge generation by narrowing the scope of evaluation. However, when a balanced approach to evaluation is taken, in which the stakeholder-informed theory driving a program guides the study design while remaining flexible and comprehensive enough to capture variation within and across sites adequately, the results are often robust data and analysis that can drive decision making. Natural-variation designs represent such an approach. In this manner political pressure may serve as a driving force for more rigorous evaluations, which have tremendous implications for social science theory.

Too often evaluation has been viewed as simply the application of social science methods to investigate social problems, thus ensuring that the flow of information between basic social science and evaluation is one way. Yet the relationship between applied research methods and evaluation described here is just a brief example of the many ways in which evaluation can serve as a nexus for improving the relevance and progress of social science. Evaluators must do more to ensure that traffic on this bridge between social science and evaluation moves freely in both directions. We can help realize the potential of evaluation by more clearly demonstrating its value and bringing knowledge gained through evaluation practice to bear not only in policies and programs, but to influence both basic social science theory and methods. With this incredible opportunity before us, evaluators should endeavor to become drivers of the exploration of human potential.

References

Chen, H. T. (2003). *Taking the perspective one step further: Providing a taxonomy for theory-driven evaluators.* Paper presented at the American Evaluation Association annual conference, Reno, NV.

Chen, H. T., & Rossi, P. (1983). Evaluating with sense: The theory-driven approach. *Evaluation Review, 7*(3), 283–302.

Donaldson, S. I. (2005). Using program theory-driven evaluation science to crack the Da Vinci Code. *New Directions for Evaluation, 106,* 65–84.

Rossi, P. H. (1987). No good applied social research goes unpunished. *Society, 25*(1), 73–79.

Sayer, R. A. (2010). *Method in social science: A realist approach.* London: Routledge.

Scriven, M. (1991). *Evaluation thesaurus* (4th ed.). Thousand Oaks, CA: Sage.

Springer, J., Sambrano, S., Sale, E., Kasim, R., Hermann, J., & Substance Abuse and Mental Health Services Administration (DHHS/PHS) (2002). *The national cross-site evaluation of high-risk youth programs: Understanding risk, protection, and substance use among high-risk youth.* Monograph Series. Rockville, MD: The Center for Substance Abuse Prevention.

Weiss, C. H. (1997). How can theory-based evaluation make greater headway? *Evaluation Review, 21*(4), 501–524.

ROBERT D. BLAGG *is a senior research associate at Evaluation Management Training Associates, Inc., whose research interests include applied research methods and the prosocial consequences of health, social, and education programs.*

Coryn, C.L.S., & Hobson, K. A. (2011). Using nonequivalent dependent variables to reduce internal validity threats in quasi-experiments: Rationale, history, and examples from practice. In S. Mathison (Ed.), *Really new directions in evaluation: Young evaluators' perspectives. New Directions for Evaluation, 131,* 31–39.

5

Using Nonequivalent Dependent Variables to Reduce Internal Validity Threats in Quasi-Experiments: Rationale, History, and Examples From Practice

Chris L.S. Coryn, Kristin A. Hobson

Abstract

Threats to the validity of inferences and conclusions regarding the effects of applied interventions have been a major dilemma for social scientists and evaluators for several decades. One mechanism for reducing threats to internal validity and improving warrants for cause-and-effect conclusions in nonrandomized investigations and evaluations is the inclusion of nonequivalent dependent variables as an element of structural design. In this chapter, the rationale for, history of, and examples from practice for using nonequivalent dependent variables to reduce internal validity threats, as well as some warrants supporting their increased use, are described. © Wiley Periodicals, Inc., and the American Evaluation Association.

Legitimate knowledge claims about causation have been a central concern among evaluators and applied researchers for several decades (Cook, Scriven, Coryn, & Evergreen, 2010). Since publication of Campbell and Stanley's (1966) *Experimental and Quasi-Experimental Designs for Research*, which was followed more than a decade later by Cook and Campbell's (1979) *Quasi-Experimentation: Design and Analysis for Field Settings,* and thereafter by Shadish, Cook, and Campbell's (2002) *Experimental and Quasi-Experimental Designs for Generalized Causal Inference*, alternative explanations for effects observed from studies of applied interventions have been the bane of practicing social scientists and evaluators. Collectively, these alternative explanations are generally known as threats to validity.

Threats to validity are (plausible) "reasons why an inference might be incorrect" (Shadish et al., 2002, p. 512). Such threats may take one or more forms, including those associated with internal, external, construct, and statistical conclusion validities. Although neither exhaustive nor mutually exclusive, most threats to validity can be situated into one or more of these four general categories. Contingent on the target of generalization, these validity threats also may manifest themselves in very different, sometimes conflicting ways, where efforts to thwart threats to one form of validity may simultaneously diminish the validity of another. In this taxonomy, internal validity is the approximate truthfulness or correctness of an inference or conclusion regarding whether a relationship between two variables is, in fact, causal. These types of validity are interdependent and can never be fully known (and only estimated based on logic and principled reasoning). Validity, therefore, is not an all-or-none proposition. Rather, it is a matter of degree and always associated with a particular purpose or use (Messick, 1989). Even so, in cause-probing investigations, internal validity typically is the primary priority, even if such knowledge claims are only localized in their generality (Campbell, 1986).

Irrespective of ideological, philosophical, and ultimately methodological disagreements and controversies (e.g., Cook et al., 2010; Coryn, 2009; Gargani, 2010; Mackie, 1980; Scriven, 1968, 1975, 1976, 2009), and, as Reichardt (2011) rightly notes, for the majority of evaluations, such inferences are about the effects of a given cause rather than questions about the cause of a given effect. From this perspective, a cause is that which precedes or produces an effect, and an effect is the difference between what occurred in the presence of a (presumed) cause and what would have occurred in its absence (i.e., counterfactual reasoning; Rubin, 1974, 2005). This view of causation is premised on manipulable causes that can be deliberately varied and that can generate reasonable approximations of the physically impossible counterfactual. Based on this logic, three conditions are necessary for causal inference (Shadish et al., 2002): (a) temporal precedence—that cause precedes effect, (b) covariation—that cause and effect vary together, and (c) absence of alternative causes—that no other plausible explanations can account for an observed treatment–outcome covariation.

Types and Sources of Potential Internal Validity Threats

Not enumerated in detail here, but essential for providing context, the most widely accepted internal validity threats are ambiguous temporal precedence, selection, history, maturation, regression, attrition, testing, instrumentation, and additive and interactive threats (see Campbell & Stanley, 1966; Cook & Campbell, 1979; and, in particular, Shadish et al., 2002). And the major focus of research design is anticipating and reducing the number and plausibility of these threats to (internal) validity. By definition, experimental designs rule out selection threats (which is the predominant bias associated with nearly all other types of designs), but not the others. Although experimental designs have received far more attention, findings from recent investigations into evaluation practice suggest that quasi-experimental designs, among others (e.g., mixed-method designs, nonexperimental designs), are far more common for evaluating social programs and other types of applied interventions than experimental designs (Christie & Fleischer, 2010; Coryn et al., 2011). For quasi-experiments, Shadish et al. (2002) enumerate three closely related principles for identifying and reducing potential alternative explanations of treatment–outcome covariation: (a) identification and study of plausible threats to internal validity, (b) primacy of control by design, and (c) coherent pattern matching.

Nonequivalent Dependent Variables

Although numerous methods and techniques (both statistical and nonstatistical) are available for reducing the number and plausibility of internal validity threats, one lesser-known and underutilized design element is nonequivalent dependent variables. A nonequivalent dependent variable is a ". . . dependent variable that is predicted *not* to change because of the treatment but is expected to respond to some or all of the contextually important internal validity threats in the same way as the target outcome" (Shadish et al., 2002, p. 509). From a measurement perspective, both dependent and nonequivalent dependent variables should consist of similar or related manifest variables or latent constructs. Otherwise, the nonequivalent dependent variable is merely arbitrary.

Rationale for Using Nonequivalent Dependent Variables to Reduce Internal Validity Threats

With the exception of Shadish et al. (2002), very few research methods textbooks refer to nonequivalent dependent variables as a means for reducing the numerous internal validity threats associated with quasi-experiments. The rationale for using nonequivalent dependent variables to reduce validity threats to quasi-experimental designs is that they provide an elegant and robust, yet simple and straightforward, means for addressing the Shadish et al. (2002) coherent pattern-matching principle. In addressing this principle, nonequivalent dependent variables can be used to represent a complex prediction of causal hypotheses that few alternative explanations could explain, and "the more complex the pattern that is successfully predicted, the less likely it is that alternative explanations could generate the same pattern . . ." (Shadish et al., 2002, p. 105).

Borrowing from, and modifying, a recent example from Reichardt (2011), consider an educational television program intended to teach children to pronounce the letters of the alphabet. Over a 12-week period the show presents the first half of the alphabet. Prior to and after viewing the show for 12 weeks children are tested (i.e., a one-group pretest–posttest design) on their ability to pronounce letters that they were exposed to (the dependent variable) as well as letters that they were not (the nonequivalent dependent variable). In terms of validity threats, several alternative explanations for any observed effect on the dependent variable would be plausible (e.g., after-school programs, parents teaching their children at home, other television programs). Even so, the same environmental and contextual validity threats would operate on both the dependent and nonequivalent dependent variables. If such validity threats were truly warranted, then they should have an effect on both variables, and, therefore, any effects would occur concomitantly. If not, then effects would be observed on the dependent variable only and not the nonequivalent dependent variable.

History and Examples of Using Nonequivalent Dependent Variables to Reduce Internal Validity Threats

Historically, and although studies using nonequivalent dependent variables appeared in the literature earlier (e.g., Robertson & Rossiter, 1976), one of the most well-known examples is McSweeny's (1978) investigation of the effect of a directory assistance charge on the number of local directory assistance calls in Cincinnati. Because the directory assistance charge was for local directory assistance only, McSweeny (1978) used the number of long-distance directory assistance calls placed as a nonequivalent dependent variable to study the effect of charging for local directory assistance on the number of calls placed for local directory assistance. Based on the a priori causal hypothesis, the charge for local directory assistance would only decrease the number of calls placed for local directory assistance, and any environmental events would affect all types of directory assistance calls and would change the numbers of local directory assistance calls as well as long-distance directory assistance calls concurrently. Plotted results, shown in Figure 5.1 (an interrupted time-series design with a nonequivalent dependent variable), suggest that only the number of local directory assistance calls changed and long-distance calls remained unchanged.

In 1980, the Philadelphia Police Department reenacted its general administrative deadly force policy that was abolished in 1974. White (2000) analyzed shooting data for on- and off-duty police officers over two periods before and after the policy revisions, 1970–1978 and 1987–1992, treating the on-duty police officers as the focal dependent variable, off-duty police

Figure 5.1. Effects of Response Costs in the Charging for Directory Assistance in Cincinnati

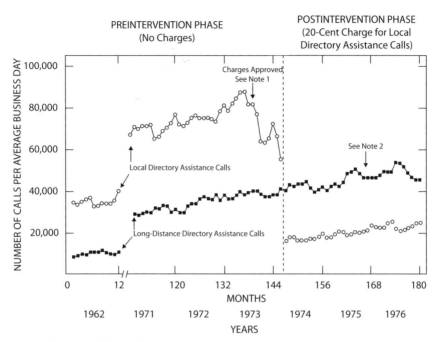

Source: McSweeny, 1978, p. 49.

officers as the nonequivalent dependent variable, and the general administrative deadly force policy as the independent variable. If changes in levels of deadly force were the result of the policy, only changes in fatal force among on-duty police officers would have occurred, whereas if the effect was due to another event, the fatal force among on- and off-duty police officers would have moved in parallel. White's (2000) analysis showed levels of deadly force between both on- and off-duty police officers moved in the same direction, but at different magnitudes, as shown in Table 5.1.

McKillip and Baldwin (1990) utilized two nonequivalent dependent variables, alcohol use and exercise, to study the effects of a sexually transmitted disease (STD) education campaign on condom usage. A college campus implemented a multimedia education campaign aimed at decreasing the prevalence of STDs through increasing condom usage. If the effect was attributable to the campaign, only college students' attitudes toward condom usage, beliefs about the consequences of using condoms inconsistently, intentions to use condoms, and discussions with friends about condom usage would have changed. If the effect was the result of another event affecting college students' attitudes, beliefs, intentions, and discussions, then alcohol

NEW DIRECTIONS FOR EVALUATION • DOI: 10.1002/ev

Table 5.1. The Nonequivalent Dependent Variables Design With Use of Deadly Force in Philadelphia Over Time by Type of Shooting (Nonelective or Elective) and Duty Status

Premeasurement	Postmeasurement	Percentage Change
Dependent variable 1	Dependent variable 1	
On-duty shootings ($n = 521$)	On-duty shootings ($n = 122$)	
Nonelective 64% (335)	Nonelective 86% (105)	+35%
Elective 36% (186)	Elective 14% (17)	−55%
Annual rate	Annual rate	
Nonelective 5.0	Nonelective 2.8	−44%
Elective 2.8	Elective 0.5	−82%
Dependent variable 2	Dependent variable 2	
Off-duty shootings ($n = 122$)	Off-duty shootings ($n = 42$)	
Nonelective 61% (74)	Nonelective 79% (43)	+30%
Elective 39% (48)	Elective 21% (9)	−46%
Annual rate	Annual rate	
Nonelective 1.1	Nonelective 0.9	−18%
Elective 0.7	Elective 0.2	−71%

Note: Annual rates are calculated per 1,000 officers using 7,388 for Time 1 (9 years) and 6,280 for Time 2 (6 years).

Source: White, 2000, p. 311.

consumption and exercise habits also would have increased at the same time as the four variables associated with increased condom usage. Moreover, if the ad campaign had no effect on the observed outcome variables, condom usage attitudes, beliefs, and intentions and discussions with friends, the outcome variables in addition to the nonequivalent dependent variables, alcohol consumption and exercise habits, would have changed in the same direction with the same magnitude. McKillip and Baldwin (1990) plotted the four condom usage variables against alcohol consumption and exercise habits and found that only beliefs supportive of condom usage and discussions with friends about condom usage changed, whereas attitudes toward and intentions to use condoms did not change (see Figures 5.2 and 5.3).

Conclusion

Combined with other structural design elements (e.g., control or comparison groups, multiple pretest or posttest observations, removed treatments), nonequivalent dependent variables offer a powerful means for improving warrants for certain cause-and-effect conclusions in nonrandomized investigations. What is more, nonequivalent dependent variables are amenable to nearly all types of research designs including, but not limited to, within-subjects designs, between-subjects designs, single-subject designs, removed treatment designs, and interrupted time-series designs. Additionally, Nimon, Zigarmi, and Allen (2011) and Pratt, McGuigan, and Katzev (2000) have

Figure 5.2. Mean Strength of Health Beliefs as a Function of the Health Topic and the Week of Observation

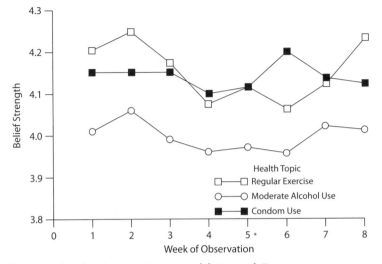

Note: The STD media education campaign occurred during week 5.

Source: McKillip and Baldwin, 1990, p. 340.

Figure 5.3. Proportion of Respondents Reporting Discussion of Health Topics With a Friend During the Current Week as a Function of the Week of Observation

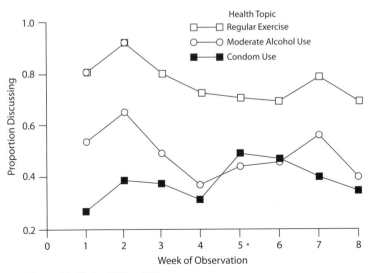

Source: McKillip and Baldwin, 1990, p. 341.

provided some empirical evidence supporting the use of retrospective pretest, which also could usefully be combined with (retrospective) non-equivalent dependent variables in many evaluation contexts given that a large majority of evaluations are retrospective rather than prospective.

References

Campbell, D. T. (1986). Relabeling internal and external validity for applied social scientists. *New Directions for Program Evaluation, 31,* 67–77.

Campbell, D. T., & Stanley, J. C. (1966). *Experimental and quasi-experimental designs for research.* Chicago, IL: Rand McNally.

Christie, C. A., & Fleischer, D. N. (2010). Insight into evaluation practice: A content analysis of designs and methods used in evaluation studies published in North American evaluation-focused journals. *American Journal of Evaluation, 31*(3), 326–346. doi: 10.1177/1098214010369170

Cook, T. D., & Campbell, D. T. (1979). *Quasi-experimentation: Design and analysis for field settings.* Chicago, IL: Rand McNally.

Cook, T. D., Scriven, M., Coryn, C. L. S., & Evergreen, S. D. H. (2010). Contemporary thinking about causation in evaluation: A dialogue with Tom Cook and Michael Scriven. *American Journal of Evaluation, 31*(1), 105–117. doi: 10.1177/ 1098214009354918

Coryn, C. L. S. (2009). Modus operandi. In L. E. Sullivan (Ed.), *The Sage glossary of the social and behavioral sciences* (p. 328). Thousand Oaks, CA: Sage.

Coryn, C. L. S., Noakes, L. A., Westine, C. D., & Schröter, D. C. (2011). A systematic review of theory-driven evaluation practice from 1990 to 2009. *American Journal of Evaluation, 32*(2), 199–226. doi: 10.1177/1098214010389321

Gargani, J. (2010). A welcome change from debate to dialogue about causality. *American Journal of Evaluation, 31*(1), 131–132. doi: 10.1177/1098214009357612

Mackie, J. L. (1980). *The cement of the universe: A study of causation.* Oxford, United Kingdom: Oxford University Press.

McKillip, J., & Baldwin, K. (1990). Evaluation of an STD education media campaign: A control construct design. *Evaluation Review, 14*(4), 331–346. doi: 10.1177 /0193841X9001400401

McSweeny, J. A. (1978). Effects of response cost on the behavior of a million persons: Charging for directory assistance in Cincinnati. *Journal of Applied Behavior Analysis, 11,* 47–51.

Messick, S. (1989). Validity. In R. L. Linn (Ed.), *Educational measurement* (3rd ed., pp. 13–103). New York, NY: Macmillan.

Nimon, K., Zigarmi, D., & Allen, J. (2011). Measures of program effectiveness based on retrospective pretest data: Are all created equal? *American Journal of Evaluation, 32*(1), 8–28. doi: 10.1177/1098214010378354

Pratt, C. C., McGuigan, W. M., & Katzev, A. R. (2000). Measuring program outcomes: Using retrospective pretest methodology. *American Journal of Evaluation, 21*(3), 341–349. doi: 10.1177/109821400002100305

Reichardt, C. S. (2011). Evaluating methods for estimating program effects. *American Journal of Evaluation, 32*(2), 246–272. doi: 10.1177/1098214011398954

Robertson, T. S., & Rossiter, J. R. (1976, February). Short-run advertising effects on children: A field study. *Journal of Marketing Research, 13,* 68–70.

Rubin, D. B. (1974). Estimating causal effects of treatments in randomized and nonrandomized studies. *Journal of Educational Psychology, 66*(5), 688–701.

Rubin, D. B. (2005). Causal inference using potential outcomes: Design, modeling, decisions. *Journal of the American Statistical Association, 100*(469), 322–331. doi: 0.1198/016214504000001880

Scriven, M. (1968). In defense of all causes. *Issues in Criminology*, 4(1), 79–81.

Scriven, M. (1975). Causation as explanation. *Nous*, 9(1), 3–16.

Scriven, M. (1976). Maximizing the power of causal investigations: The modus operandi method. In G. V. Glass (Ed.), *Evaluation studies review annual* (Vol. 1, pp. 101–118). Beverly Hills, CA: Sage.

Scriven, M. (2009). Demythologizing causation and evidence. In S. I. Donaldson, C. A. Christie, & M. M. Mark (Eds.), *What counts as credible evidence in applied research and evaluation practice?* (pp. 134–152). Thousand Oaks, CA: Sage.

Shadish, W. R., Cook, T. D., & Campbell, D. T. (2002). *Experimental and quasi-experimental designs for generalized causal inference.* Boston, MA: Houghton Mifflin.

White, M. D. (2000). Assessing the impact of administrative policy on use of deadly force by on- and off-duty police. *Evaluation Review*, 24(3), 295–318. doi: 10.1177 /0193841X0002400303

CHRIS L. S. CORYN is the director of the Interdisciplinary PhD in Evaluation program and assistant professor of Evaluation, Measurement, and Research at Western Michigan University.

KRISTIN A. HOBSON is a doctoral student in the Interdisciplinary PhD in Evaluation program at Western Michigan University.

Evergreen, S.D.H. (2011). Eval + comm. In S. Mathison (Ed.), *Really new directions in evaluation: Young evaluators' perspectives. New Directions for Evaluation, 131,* 41–45.

6

Eval + Comm

Stephanie D. H. Evergreen

Abstract

Graphic design has a role in securing the attention and engagement of the reader, a way of making complicated data a more digestible cognitive aid, but it has been almost entirely ignored until quite recently in evaluation. The author argues that the professionalism of evaluators and evaluation practice will require an evolution in the way evaluators talk about our work. The author describes a number of models and sources of inspiration for becoming more mindful communicators. © Wiley Periodicals, Inc., and the American Evaluation Association.

The future of evaluation may not include teleportation and mind-reading software, but I am fairly certain it will include advances in the way we communicate with each other and our clients. The average length of an evaluation report in the Western Michigan University Evaluation Center's library is 175 pages. Granted, size alone doesn't determine engagement. But the page after page of solid black text does indicate how unlikely clients are to read the report end to end. Evaluators have the bad habit of making our reporting terribly boring—not the content (quite the contrary) but the communication.

The disconnect lies between our desire to have our findings used and our methods of presenting them. Generally, evaluators haven't incorporated theories of information processing in reporting. But understanding how written reports are picked up, read, and digested or how audiences comprehend a slideshow is increasingly available to us. Other fields, like applied statistics, employ the basic tenets of visual processing theory and graphic design to make their work more readily understood and useful. This chapter is a primer on visual cognition and graphic design strategies that will increase the likelihood that our findings will be understood and remembered long after the invoice has cleared.

Visual Processing Theory and Evaluation

Today's graphic design practice relies on theories explaining visual perception to create communications that better engage viewers. Indeed, scholars debate whether graphic design ought to be a branch of visual science (Poyner, 2010) because of the latter's fundamental role at the core of all communication in graphic design. Visual processing theory describes how the brain interprets what the eyes see. It operates in three phases (preattention, working memory, and long-term memory) that guide graphic designers toward arranging information with a better chance of being encoded in long-term memory. For evaluators, these skills can help us better support understanding and decision-making.

Phase One: Preattention

We have historically relied on phase-one visual processing to scope the horizon, looking for food or mates or danger. Humans are adept at noticing tiny changes in our environment, patterns or abnormalities, so much so that we don't have to be cognitively engaged to do it. When we are simply scanning for things that pop out, we are using our natural preattentive function. It is what is at play when something catches our eye.

As evaluators, we should be tapping into this function more often: color, alignment, motion, orientation, and size will grab attention, that is, preattention (Malamed, 2009; Ware, 2008; Wolfe & Horowitz, 2004). Probably the most valuable graphic-design intervention an evaluator can administer in phase one is to create a hierarchy of information for the reader. Typically, written reports have little variation, save the smattering of charts and tables. By creating a hierarchy of information, the evaluator uses graphic design techniques to point out what part of the report is most important for the reader, what is next most important, and so on. Sometimes preattention is cued in a hierarchy through headings, where typeface or size can indicate a change in topic. We can extend the use of phase-one attributes by using outdent or color to highlight key findings so they are quickly located by a busy reader.

Charts and graphs are also eye-catchers. Given this elevated stature, evaluators would do well to reserve graphs to emphasize what is important in the report, rather than use a graph or table for every question asked on the survey, for example. This way, the reader will be cued to the most critical information. The point here is to use preattentive features judiciously. Too little will not pull in a busy nonprofit executive. Too much will be seen as garish, driving readers away from engagement in phase two.

Phase Two: Working Memory

To get things to stick in our clients' brains for a long time, we have to help the information land in long-term memory. But to get there, it must pass the working memory roadblock, phase two. Attributes noticed in phase one, having gotten the attention of the reader, are held in working memory. This phase is where we wrestle with information to process it and stick it in long-term memory. But research shows we can only hold three to five chunks in working memory at any time, and that even varies by the context (Cowan, 2000; Xu & Chun, 2006).

Working memory is weak. When it is distracted or overloaded, some chunks of information are dropped and misunderstanding or frustration results. To reduce the risk of overload, the designer often predigests some of the information. Think of how a graph represents some mental processing that would have had to take place in the viewer's brain if she was simply reading the information as gray narrative. Similarly, the designer "prechunks," essentially allowing more information into working memory than otherwise possible. Other strategies include making the graphic object as clear as possible, without unnecessary lines or color changes. Choosing typefaces that best enhance legibility is another strategy evaluators can use to make our work more user-friendly. For example, serif fonts best support readability and recall of information (Samara, 2007; Wheildon, 2005).

Our applied-statistician colleagues can also help us take visual processing into account to improve our graphs. For instance, the brain more accurately processes position along a common scale than color, particularly when asking a reader to hold those bits of information in working memory in order to draw comparisons (Cleveland & McGill, 1984a). For example, pie charts are poor supports for comparison-based judgments because the brain isn't able to compare triangular-shaped areas accurately (Few, 2009; Tufte, 2001).

Phase Three: Long-Term Memory

With the right cognitive load in working memory, objects, their attributes, and their message can make it to phase three, where they are encoded into long-term memory (Lockhart & Craik, 1990; Malamed, 2009; Ware, 2008). Once there, new information is incorporated into existing mental schemas, or networks of information stored in the human brain. This is when comprehension and cognition occur.

Again, our graph-happy colleagues have already done the groundwork to demonstrate how graphic design affects comprehension. They have shown, for example, how interpretation and recall are supported if one color is used among otherwise gray bars instead of a range of colors or gradation (Cleveland & McGill, 1984b; Few, 2009). Additional visual processing theory-based principles used in graphing include using faint gridlines (when used at all) so as not to distract from the data lines, avoiding line patterns or texture that cause optical illusions, and placing associated text and graphic within one eye span.

Similarly, statisticians have tested visual processing's strategic implications for questionnaire design as a way to explain how layout contributes to measurement error (Stern, Dillman, & Smyth, 2007). For example, tests of proximity showed that when response options were grouped and cued with headings and good spacing, completed responses improved by almost 30% (Smyth, Dillman, Christian, & Stern, 2006). Bad spacing often caused one response option to stand out and led to its disproportionate selection (Christian & Dillman, 2004). Respondents were less likely to complete a questionnaire if the text was "reversed out," where light-colored words were placed on a dark background (Whitcomb & Porter, 2004). As a body of research, this shows that communication and reader comprehension is impacted by graphic design choices.

The developments in data displays and questionnaire formatting demonstrate that a visual language communicates beyond the words composing the items, response options, and data labels. Do you sense this topic creeping ever closer to evaluation? Credibility can be lost with poor graphic design (Tufte, 1997). Evaluators have a responsibility to make their work as clear and accessible as possible, both to enhance the evaluation's credibility and to encourage the use of evaluation in program change.

Not too far in our future our evaluation presentations will be so powerful our clients will find them literally unforgettable, because we have so integrated strategies steeped in visual processing theory. Using graphic design speeds the acquisition of information and reduces misinterpretation, two outcomes we want for clients reading our evaluation findings. It is another responsible step evaluators can take to encourage the use of our findings. Although comprehension, retention, and recall may not (yet) predict use of our results, it sure is a step in the right direction.

References

Christian, L. M., & Dillman, D. A. (2004). The influence of graphical and symbolic language manipulations on response to self-administered questions. *Public Opinion Quarterly, 68*(1), 57–80.

Cleveland, W. S., & McGill, R. (1984a). Graphical perception: Theory, experimentation, and application to the development of graphical methods. *Journal of the American Statistical Association, 79*(387), 531–554.

Cleveland, W. S., & McGill, R. (1984b). The many faces of a scatterplot. *Journal of the American Statistical Association, 79*(388), 807–822.

Cowan, N. (2000). The magical number 4 in short-term memory: A reconsideration of mental storage capacity. *Behavioral and Brain Sciences, 24*, 87–185.

Few, S. (2009). *Now you see it: Simple visualization techniques for quantitative analysis.* Oakland, CA: Analytics Press.

Lockhart, R. S., & Craik, F. I. M. (1990). Levels of processing: A retrospective commentary on a framework for memory research. *Canadian Journal of Psychology, 44*(1), 87–112.

Malamed, C. (2009). *Visual language for designers: Principles for creating graphics that people understand.* Beverly, MA: Rockport.

Poyner, R. (2010). *Out of the studio: Graphic design history and visual studies.* Retrieved from http://ow.ly/3UlLD

Samara, T. (2007). *Design elements: A graphic style manual.* Beverly, MA: Rockport Press.

Smyth, J. D., Dillman, D. A., Christian, L. M., & Stern, M. J. (2006). Effects of using visual design principles to group response options in web surveys. *International Journal of Internet Science, 1*(1), 6–16.

Stern, M. J., Dillman, D. A., & Smyth, J. D. (2007). Visual design, order effects, and respondent characteristics in a self-administered survey. *Survey Research Methods, 1*(3), 121–138.

Tufte, E. R. (1997). *Visual explanations: Images and quantities, evidence and narrative.* Chesire, CT: Graphics Press.

Tufte, E. R. (2001). *The visual display of quantitative information* (2nd ed.). Chesire, CT: Graphics Press.

Ware, C. (2008). *Visual thinking for design.* Burlington, MA: Morgan Kaufmann.

Wheildon, C. (2005). *Type and layout: Are you communicating or just making pretty shapes?* Mentone, Australia: The Worsley Press.

Whitcomb, M. E., & Porter, S. R. (2004). E-mail contacts: A test of complex graphical designs in survey research. *Social Science Computer Review, 22*(3), 370–376.

Wolfe, J. M., & Horowitz, T. S. (2004). What attributes guide the deployment of visual attention and how do they do it? *Nature, 5,* 1–7.

Xu, Y., & Chun, M. M. (2006). Dissociable neural mechanisms supporting visual short-term memory for objects. *Nature, 440,* 91–95.

STEPHANIE D. H. EVERGREEN *runs Evergreen Evaluation, an evaluation and communication consulting firm, and is a doctoral candidate in the Interdisciplinary PhD in Evaluation program at Western Michigan University.*

NEW DIRECTIONS FOR EVALUATION • DOI: 10.1002/ev

Galloway, K. L. (2011). Focus groups in the virtual world: Implications for the future of evaluation. In S. Mathison (Ed.), *Really new directions in evaluation: Young evaluators' perspectives. New Directions for Evaluation, 131,* 47–51.

7

Focus Groups in the Virtual World: Implications for the Future of Evaluation

Kristin L. Galloway

Abstract

Focus groups are an important methodology in evaluation, and with the availability of new technology in communication the options for how to perform focus groups are growing. The author describes the experience of using focus groups electronically or online, and provides an illustration of conducting a focus group in an online chat room with international participants. Various strengths and weaknesses of focus groups in alternative mediums are identified, and questions are raised for using virtual focus groups in the future. © Wiley Periodicals, Inc., and the American Evaluation Association.

Second to the survey, one of the most common data-collection methods in program evaluation is the interview, which can be one-on-one or within a focus group (Spaulding, 2008). Focus groups are beneficial in that they enhance disclosure, facilitate openness, validate common experiences, provide access to unique concepts and language not available through quantitative methods, and allow participants freedom to follow their own agenda with some moderation from the researcher (Wilkinson, 2005). Although the prevailing methodology for focus groups has been to gather groups of individuals face-to-face within a physical proximity, the advent and rise of various audio and video technologies has led some researchers to experiment with adjusted focus-group methods over long distances through electronic mediums (Kenney, 2005).

Over the past 20 years, researchers have reported on focus groups using alternate methods, illustrating the benefits and drawbacks and asking further questions. White and Thomson (1995) conducted focus groups through audio teleconferencing. They were initially concerned about how anonymous focus groups (not face-to-face but just using voices) could limit the nonverbal cues available to researchers. However, they point out that face-to-face groups can be expensive and logistically difficult to organize, and that an anonymous group is potentially perceived as less threatening and more likely to promote discussion with sensitive topics. Campbell et al. (2001) conducted face-to-face and online focus groups on the same topic and compared results; they found similar data and themes from both groups. They also noted that participants in face-to-face groups were more likely to hold back from reporting sensitive information, but typing in the on-line groups led to shortened or omitted comments that might otherwise have been voiced. Therefore, although responses between types of focus groups may look different, they can generally produce similar information. Barbour (2007) found that individuals are less likely to dominate electronic groups, because of the lack of visual stimuli and status cues, which might negate some concerns about matching group members based on targeted homogeneity variables.

Stewart and Williams (2005) provided a very thorough summary and examples of uses of electronic media for focus groups, and some of the benefits and drawbacks of the various options. They define the parameters of an online focus group (not data mining) and identify the differences between asynchronous groups (collecting and sharing inputs one at a time over a longer span of time, such as using e-mail) and synchronous groups (real-time sharing and processing of multiple inputs, such as using chat rooms). They also discuss the concern that the speed of synchronous groups may require different or more advanced skills in moderation.

An Illustration of Virtual Focus Groups in Evaluation

From 2008 through 2009, I conducted a program evaluation on a train-the-trainer program conducted by the Community Stress Prevention Center (CSPC) (2011) in Kiryat Shmona, Israel. Trainers from the CSPC worked with first responders in both Israel and Switzerland. (For information on the full evaluation, see Galloway, 2010.) A posttraining focus group was conducted in English (all trainers were proficient in verbal and written English) in an on-line chat room with the use of AoL (America Online) chat with the trainers and evaluators communicating from three sites (United States, Switzerland, and Israel). In researching remote, international, or other hard-to-reach populations, creative methods are required for data gathering under multiple constraints. Face-to-face focus groups were not an option, because

NEW DIRECTIONS FOR EVALUATION • DOI: 10.1002/ev

of monetary and time limitations. I considered the pros and cons of using audio or video teleconferencing versus online written communication. Although the U.S. site had video teleconference access, it was not as easily accessible to international participants.

I was concerned about some risks with the voice-only teleconferencing option. If multiple people are speaking at once, there is a possibility that data would be lost. Particularly when conducting discussions among English as second language speakers, there is a high potential for misunderstanding due to accents and participants missing information because of the pace of the conversation. Conducting a focus group in an online chat-room format negated many of the downsides to an audio discussion over the phone or video device. Only a computer and internet access is required, which is conveniently available and familiar to a growing population of people around the world. Participants from multiple locations can simultaneously type their comments, which can be automatically recorded in a written transcript for analysis, avoiding the need for audio recording and transcription. Online written responses open up the possibility for multiple perspectives to be presented in real time and recorded on the screen for the participants' reference. As moderator, I found this synchronous format manageable by keeping the participant numbers low and also having a comoderator to help monitor comments and keep us on track. Also, depending on the written literacy of the participants, missing information because of spoken accents and speed of verbal discussion may be less likely.

With some possible benefits come potential drawbacks: The nonverbal behaviors of the participants could not be observed. Facial expressions and body posture provide emotional immediacy that can be followed up on by the evaluator. There is also the possibility in online focus groups that participants might attempt to multitask during the group or hold side conversations, moving their full attention away from the focus-group tasks without the knowledge of the rest of the group or evaluators. Despite any drawbacks, based on my experience using an online focus group, it was the best option given the unique circumstances of the evaluation. Feedback from participants was also very positive. Because the group took place in various time zones and on a Sunday (which can be a work day depending on the setting and culture), the participants could access the group from their desk at work, at an internet café, or from the privacy of their home, based on their needs. Such convenience factors could maximize the amount of participation and types of participants in other similar groups.

Some Concerns Arising From the Virtual Focus Groups

Concerns that might have been present when collecting data on-line are security, maintaining confidentiality, and overall ethical considerations for minimizing harm to participants. Depending on the medium used and nature of the network, evaluators may be limited in their ability to guarantee that someone who is a nonapproved participant cannot access the focus-group discussion. Thorough informed consent from participants and taking steps to set up the most secure communication link possible is still a crucial responsibility of the evaluator. Another area of informed consent includes developing and posting rules of engagement for the group, and how the evaluator is going to moderate participation. Focus-group participants have the power to walk away, but as the initiator of the on-line groups, the moderator has more power to switch off individual participants, and deciding beforehand when and why to do this is recommended. A possible ethical issue is that evaluators may have limited power and information to intervene or follow up in risky or sensitive situations when participants are remote or anonymous. If a participant indicates suicidal or homicidal ideation and then leaves the group, what are the evaluators' options for follow-up and promoting safety? Perhaps requiring contact information for participants in on-line groups discussing sensitive topics is ideal.

New Technologies for Virtual Focus Groups

The possibilities and options for evaluators using focus groups is growing, and continued use of new technologies with focus groups and sharing feedback from different platforms is essential for future researchers to expand in this area. Companies such as Skype (2011) created a platform for inexpensive and simple-to-use video teleconferencing that is increasingly accessible to anyone in the world with an internet connection. Computer software that automatically translates written and spoken words into different languages could help break down barriers to conducting focus groups more frequently with international participants. Computer software that assists in analyzing transcripts for themes can help the researcher with time and efficiency (Matheson, 2005). Programs using online avatar technology are currently used more prolifically for a variety of applications. Companies such as In World Solutions (2011) have created virtual avatar environments to expand and optimize mental health treatments in multiple settings through rapid engagement, overcoming emotional barriers, and working with clients remotely. The U.S. military has been using similar virtual reality to facilitate training and treat posttraumatic stress disorder through immersion in remote environments (Wilson, 2008). Stewart and Williams (2005) stated that avatar groups might be more beneficial than other online groups because of the participants' expression of immediate physical and emotional reactions through the avatar. However, these reactions are still controlled secondhand by the participant, and may not reflect the immediate reaction that one might see in a face-to-face setting. Further exploration is needed on how the added avatar component benefits or complicates a focus group.

Sometimes, the ideal research design and data-gathering methods for evaluating a program and performing focus groups are not always logistically possible given budget and time restrictions, international scope and location, and language barriers. Expanding the use of online focus groups can help overcome some of those barriers. Currently, there is not a clear best strategy for conducting focus groups online; however, options can be chosen by weighing the benefits and drawbacks with each individual evaluation. Some areas of focus in the fields of psychology and program evaluation in the new millennium include promoting diversity and working internationally, understanding and adapting to how technology can broaden and complicate operations, and incorporating empirically supported practices. The proliferation of online focus-group research will help promote these aims by reaching more diverse populations and adding to our knowledge and guidelines of what works best with focus-group methods online and in virtual worlds.

References

Barbour, R. S. (2007). *Doing focus groups*. London, United Kingdom: Sage.

Campbell, M. K., Meier, A., Carr, C., Enga, Z., James, A. S., Reedy, J., & Zheng, B. (2001). Health behavior changes after colon cancer: A comparison of findings from face-to-face and on-line focus groups, *Family and Community Health, 24*(3), 88–103.

The Community Stress Prevention Center website. (2011). Retrieved from http://www.icspc.org

Galloway, K. L. (2010). *Evaluation of a first responder train the trainer program for Israeli and Swiss firefighters* (Unpublished doctoral dissertation). Wright State University, Dayton, OH.

In World Solutions. (2011). Retrieved from http://www.InWorldSolutions.com

Kenney, A. J. (2005). Interaction in cyberspace: An online focus group. *Journal of Advanced Nursing, 49*(4), 414–422.

Matheson, J. L. (2005). Computer-aided qualitative data analysis software: General issues for family therapy researchers. In D. H. Sprenkle & F. P. Percy (Eds.), *Research methods in family therapy* (2nd ed., pp. 119–135). New York, NY: Guilford Press.

Skype. (2011). Retrieved from http://www.skype.com

Spaulding, D. T. (2008). *Program evaluation in practice: Core concepts and examples for discussion and analysis*. San Francisco, CA: Jossey-Bass.

Stewart, K., & Williams, M. (2005). Researching online populations: The use of online focus groups for social research. *Qualitative Research, 5*(4), 395–416.

White, G. E., & Thomson, A. N. (1995). Anonymized focus groups as a research tool for health professionals. *Qualitative Health Research, 5*, 256–260.

Wilkinson, S. (2005). Using focus groups: Exploring the meanings of health and illness. In. J. Miles & P. Gilbert (Eds.), *A handbook of research methods for clinical and health psychology* (pp. 79–94). New York, NY: Oxford University Press.

Wilson, C. (2008, April 9). *Avatars, virtual reality technology, and the U.S. military: Emerging policy issues*. CRS Report for Congress. Order Code RS22857.

KRISTIN L. GALLOWAY is a clinical psychology intern in Dayton, OH.

Bheda, D. (2011). En"gendering" evaluation: Feminist evaluation but "I am NOT a feminist!" In S. Mathison (Ed.), *Really new directions in evaluation: Young evaluators' perspectives. New Directions for Evaluation, 131*, 53–58.

8

En"gendering" Evaluation: Feminist Evaluation but "I Am NOT a Feminist!"

Divya Bheda

Abstract

The author explores the information gained through interviewing 13 feminist evaluators to explore (a) possible reasons why many evaluators—who draw from feminist principles and research—choose not to identify as "feminist" in their evaluation practice and scholarship and (b) the potential gains and losses to not locating themselves as feminist evaluators. © Wiley Periodicals, Inc., and the American Evaluation Association.

In the last 2 years, through my participation in the Feminist Issues topical interest group of the American Evaluation Association (AEA), I found that feminist evaluators expressed frustration on two levels: (a) the lack of acknowledgment that feminist evaluation is a legitimate evaluation approach (e.g., in Alkin & Christie, 2004), and (b) the overt and subversive resistance many feminist evaluators face from peers, clients, stakeholders, and funders in different contexts—the eye rolls, the uncomfortable laughter, the mocking—when they use the term *feminist* within their evaluation work. (See Patton, 2002; Podems, 2010; Sielbeck-Bowen, Brisolara, Seigart, Tischler, and Whitmore, 2002, for an understanding of

The author would like to extend sincere thanks to Dr. Ron Beghetto for suggestions on an earlier draft.

feminist evaluation. Also see Harding, 2004; Collins, 2000; Jaggar, 2008; Smith, 1999, to understand feminist contributions to epistemology and methodology in research.)

Simultaneously, I also realized a discrepancy existed in that a large number of people actually seemed to be doing feminist evaluative work, yet did not name themselves or their evaluation work as *feminist*. In this article I explore this discrepancy by drawing from interviews I conducted with 13 feminist evaluators. In doing so, I hope to highlight the barriers faced by these evaluators, and the potential personal and professional losses and gains involved in identifying one's work as *feminist*.

In summarizing these interviews I attempt to represent the knowledge, experiences, thoughts, and perspectives shared with me. Given that I too am a feminist evaluator, I hereafter refer to those I interviewed as *colleagues*. I have represented their voices in quotes without specific identifiers, other than a letter and a random number (e.g., C1, C2) to help distinguish among the different voices. The purpose of engaging in this form of representation is for the reader to pay attention to their experiences as opposed to attributing meaning and intention to what they say based on who they are as individuals.

Barriers to Using the Term *Feminist* in Evaluation

Personal Concerns

Numerous personal identity concerns seemed to influence my colleagues' decisions not to call themselves feminist evaluators. The word *feminist* is a historically politically loaded label that some of my colleagues struggle to identify with. "Could one be feminist if one were a man?" [C2]. "I am not sure I would qualify as a 'feminist'. . ." [C9]. Perhaps a lack of familiarity with the feminist scholarship resulted in a hesitation and ambivalence for some of my colleagues in their willingness to be identified as *feminist* because it forced them to question whether they were being true feminists or not.

A second common concern among my colleagues was a tendency for feminist evaluators to "impose their dominant values as white, western, neoliberal, middle-class women, on women of color" [C12] within the local U.S. context and on third-world women in the international context— without considering "negative impacts of imposing their emancipatory agendas and values" [C2] on others. "It is colonizing . . . imperialistic . . . How can you be a feminist evaluator if you are not self-reflexive about it!" [C13] exclaimed one colleague in frustration. This causes some of my colleagues (especially those of color) to be careful about who they ally with and how they use the term *feminist* because they do not want their identity to be co-opted within a dominant understanding of feminism that excludes and marginalizes these colleagues' intersecting racial and ethnic identity concerns. (See also Mohanty, 1997, 2003 for a similar representation of these concerns.)

Political Concerns

Some colleagues described how, in private, they identified themselves and their work as *feminist* but strategically choose whether and when they will publicly attribute their work as *feminist* because of having negative experiences, and resistance to identifying as *feminist*. All my colleagues, including those who did not see themselves as feminist evaluators, used words such as "strident," "radical," "bra-burning," or "man-hating" to describe how others perceived them and their work when they did identify as *feminist*. One colleague stated, "go through the Eval Talk archives. . .search 'feminist' to see some of the interactions . . . people attack you . . . without even a basic understanding of what it really is . . ." [C1].

Colleagues agreed that using the word *feminist* is often isolating and "too political" [C4] for many people because "it rocks the boat" [C10]. One identified the "conservative, right-wing political force" [C8] within the United States that has been and continues to be dominant in framing the word *feminist* as being "anti-woman, anti-family, and anti-man" [C4], thereby marginalizing them if they choose to identify as such. "It feels like those who practice evaluation within the academic community can use the word feminist . . . it is a privilege" [C1] because they "interact with people who know . . . feminist scholarship and ideas . . ." [C8]. "Those of us who rely on referrals . . . work as independent consultants . . . especially in rural areas . . . or as part of evaluation agencies . . . we decide to use the term based on how receptive we think our clients, stakeholder communities, funders, etc. are . . ." [C3].

Within the international context, colleagues identified "patriarchal systems, governments, and cultures" [C5] that resist any overt reference to feminist principles because it challenges the current power structure. In response, some colleagues had strategically reframed their evaluation work as being about "social justice goals" [C11] or "human rights" [C6] to gain political entry and access within these projects and contexts: "Social justice is more inclusive . . . not just women or gender . . . allows for a deeper structural transformation" [C11].

As illustrated by the example above, many of my colleagues resort to using other terminology to gain entry within evaluation endeavors to begin engaging in the social justice work they are committed to as feminist evaluators. Table 8.1 provides an overview of alternative terms and labels used instead of *feminist* to engage with stakeholders and peers. The one instance where my colleagues did use the term *feminist* was when they knew that all the people in the evaluation endeavor were familiar with feminist scholarship and social justice work.

Losses and Gains to Not Using *Feminist* in Feminist Evaluation

Not using the term *feminist* meant, "we are able to do our work. Ultimately that is what matters . . . whether we use the term feminist or not" [C7]. When asked about what is lost, many colleagues said "community," describing

Table 8.1. Alternative Labels for *Feminist*

Labels/Terms Used by Evaluators[a]	Access/Entry Within Stakeholder Groups[b]	Reasons for Ease or Difficulty Level of Access/Entry as Mentioned by Feminist Evaluators (Per Data Analysis Themes)
Women's issues	Easy access—least political	Invokes paternal, savior attitudes; nonthreatening to power structure at play
Gender issues/ gender responsive	Allows access—less political, though the term *gender* is sometimes seen as political	Perceived as enabling deeper understanding of what is going on differently in terms of program impact and outcomes for the different genders; more neutral because it seems inclusive
Women's rights/ human rights	Difficult access (potential barrier)—more political	Political, legal, and economic sanction implications are incentives to preserve rights and ensure no violations, thus enabling access
Feminist	Most difficult access (usually a barrier)—most political	Carries multiple negative connotations; cultural and systemic resistance because of its political meaning and overt analysis of power; seen as imposing white, western, middle-class, neoliberal values of feminism and women's liberation and emancipation in third-world and women-of-color social programming contexts

[a]The particular labels listed in the above table arose from this specific set of interviews. Other terms may exist.

[b]This hierarchy is based on the specific set of interviews and my *colleagues'* rating/understanding of the same. It may vary based on context.

having to "hide who we are and where we draw inspiration from" [C10], and that was "tiring, exhausting and isolating" [C1]. Colleagues also explained that doing so silenced the core of who they were:

> We are catering to the system . . . and feeding the same oppressive power structures by being silent [C8].

> We lose the opportunity to deepen our own learning and understanding . . . having enriching discussions . . . lead to better evaluative skills and greater social justice goals . . . [C11].

> . . . we are not building . . . sustaining our . . . tradition nor taking our own work forward [C5].

When asked about what the evaluation community gained and lost, colleagues primarily described what was lost:

> Nobody will know that many of the evaluation approaches use feminist methods and principles . . . [C7].

Feminist research and scholarship created the space and thinking for people to go behind that black box into households . . . into the lives of people . . . a lot of participatory qualitative methods used in the social sciences . . . evaluation . . . today have their origins in feminist research [C12].

The biggest loss for the field, however, as described by my colleagues, was the loss of understanding and use of the concept of "*reflexivity*"—of evaluators being able to be self-reflective and accountable in their own practice. Additionally, "we lose: the value of lived experience and subjectivity" [C2]; ". . . a lens and framework to unpack power for social change. . ." [C8]; and "the meaning and hard work of the feminist scholars that we have built our methods and principles . . . that we premise our work on" [C7].

Next Steps: Is It Just a Word? Does It Matter?

When I asked my colleagues about whether *feminist* still held meaning and significance for evaluators and the evaluation community, they explained: "It is ultimately just a word you know . . . critical, reflexive . . . we use multiple approaches anyway . . ." [C13]. "I don't want a word to stop me from doing the actual work. The work is feminist still in its spirit . . ." [C4]. However, every one of them affirmed the need to retain use of *feminist*:

If we give up on feminist . . . work . . . is diluted [C1].

Language is important . . . we need to educate more people you know. The more we identify our work as being feminist, if nowhere else but in the writing-up of our work . . . it would still help don't you think? [C3].

The next generation of evaluators getting educated will . . . learn about this approach like the way other . . . fields have . . . incorporated feminist perspectives and influences into their . . . body of work [C8].

if we give up on the word then . . . we would be catering to the power structures in our own field . . . [C6].

As feminist evaluators, we must understand that we are facing the same resistance and marginalization . . . that feminist researchers and theorists faced in the sciences, social sciences . . . [C7].

We need . . . education about feminist scholarship so that we all grow . . . understand . . . appreciate . . . learn from what feminist approaches have to offer . . . otherwise we will continue to be marginalized and we continue to marginalize ourselves within the evaluation community [C12].

Even as I end this chapter, the Feminist Issues topical interest group gets ready to put together yet another gender-responsive evaluation workshop. As my colleagues do what they can to enable education around feminist evaluation, I—in solidarity—say: "I am en'gendering' evaluation. I engage in feminist evaluation and I AM a feminist!"

References

Alkin, M., & Christie, C. (2004). An evaluation theory tree. In M. Alkin (Ed.), *Evaluation roots: Tracing theorists' views and influences*. Thousand Oaks, CA: Sage.

Collins, P. H. (2000). *Black feminist thought: Knowledge, consciousness, and the politics of empowerment*. New York, NY: Routledge.

Harding, S. G. (2004). *The feminist standpoint theory reader: Intellectual and political controversies*. New York, NY: Routledge.

Jaggar, A. M. (2008). *Just methods: An interdisciplinary feminist reader*. Boulder, CO: Paradigm.

Mohanty, C. T. (1997). Under western eyes: feminist scholarship and colonial discourses. *Cultural Politics, 11*, 255–277.

Mohanty, C. T. (2003). "Under western eyes" revisited: Feminist solidarity through anticapitalist struggles. *Signs, 28*(2), 499–535.

Patton, M. Q. (2002). Feminist, yes, but is it evaluation? *New Directions for Evaluation, 96*, 97–108.

Podems, D. (2010). Feminist evaluation and gender approaches: There's a difference? *Journal of MultiDisciplinary Evaluation, 6*(14). Retrieved from http://survey.ate.wmich .edu/jmde/index.php/jmde_1

Sielbeck-Bowen, K. A., Brisolara, S., Seigart, D., Tischler, C., & Whitmore, E. (2002). Exploring feminist evaluation: The ground from which we rise. *New Directions for Evaluation, 96*, 3–8.

Smith, L. T. (1999). *Decolonizing methodologies: Research and indigenous peoples*. London: Zed Books.

DIVYA BHEDA is a doctoral candidate in the College of Education's Critical and Socio-cultural Studies Program, University of Oregon, whose research interests include institutional responsiveness, decolonizing education, and feminist evaluation.

NEW DIRECTIONS FOR EVALUATION • DOI: 10.1002/ev

Schlueter, D. F. (2011). New evaluators addressing health disparities through community-based evaluation. In S. Mathison (Ed.), *Really new directions in evaluation: Young evaluators' perspectives. New Directions for Evaluation, 131,* 59–64.

9

New Evaluators Addressing Health Disparities Through Community-Based Evaluation

Dara F. Schlueter

Abstract

The author explores challenges in assessing health issues among ethnic and racially diverse populations, especially those related to a lack of long-standing relationships with community leaders, knowledge about the community and its needs, and sufficient funding to maintain lasting engagement within the communities of interest. One of the overarching goals of Healthy People 2010, to eliminate health disparities in the United States, has awarded much attention to the correlation between race/ethnicity and persistent and increasing health disparities among U.S. populations. Approaches for implementing and evaluating health interventions designed to address these disparities must be community based in order to identify feasible strategies for improving processes and outcomes among populations of interest. © Wiley Periodicals, Inc., and the American Evaluation Association.

Health Disparities in the United States

Although the overall health and life expectancy of Americans have improved over the past several decades, different social groups experience varying levels of health in the United States (Braveman, 2006; Giles & Liburd, 2007). Although there are many proposed definitions for health disparities, one common one is that health disparities reflect conditions that are unjust, unfair, preventable, and directly related to the historical and current social, economic, environmental, and political experiences of these groups (Centers for Disease Control and Prevention [CDC], 2009). These differences in health status and outcomes across social groups (whether defined by race or ethnicity, gender, sexual orientation, income, education, disability, or geographic location) may result from the differing social conditions among these groups and their impact on each group's susceptibility to certain health conditions, severity of those conditions, and survival rates (Giles & Liburd, 2007). Because groups currently experiencing poorer health status and outcomes are expected to grow in the next decade because of demographic changes, magnifying these differences and impacting our nation's health as a whole, it is imperative that health disparities is a major focus for our nation's public health efforts (CDC, 2009).

Health disparities among minority groups in the United States are well documented in public health literature and have been widely addressed on the national level. Perhaps the most persistent and apparent health disparities exist among racial and ethnic minority groups. One community-based effort that has been implemented at the national level is the CDC's Racial and Ethnic Approaches to Community Health (REACH 2010) initiative, which provides funding to a number of community-based interventions across the nation that aim to reduce racial and ethnic health disparities. Launched in 2007, the REACH 2010 program has a focus on six health concerns that disproportionately affect racial and ethnic minority groups, including infant mortality, cancer screening and management, cardiovascular disease, diabetes, HIV/AIDS, and immunization (CDC, 2009). Local programs funded through REACH 2010 have already demonstrated significant improvements in the health of racial and ethnic minority populations served, including reductions in disparities related to cholesterol screening, hypertension, diabetes, and various health behaviors (e.g., cigarette smoking) (CDC, 2009).

Community-Based Evaluation

Community-based evaluation is a buzz phrase in the field of public health. Oftentimes, descriptions of community-based evaluation and research rest on the commonly utilized academic approach of community-based participatory research (CBPR). As noted by Israel et al. (cited by Ahmed, Beck, Maurana, & Newton, 2004), CBPR is an approach to public health research characterized by collaborative partnership between those affected by the health issue of interest (community members, organizational representatives, and researchers) throughout every aspect of the research process. This approach ideally involves education and social action to affect change in the community setting, and promises to directly benefit the individuals studied and the communities in which they live. CBPR also includes the ongoing exchange of information, skills, and resources that result in a sustained impact on the communities in which research is being conducted (Ahmed et al., 2004). In addition to public health, CBPR is an approach that has proven successful in several social science fields, including sociology and anthropology, and has been widely accepted in the United States and internationally.

Community-based approaches to evaluation are likely the cornerstone for strong evaluation efforts addressing racial and ethnic health disparities. In addition to involving the community in every stage of the evaluation process, community-based approaches involve field testing of interventions and pilot programs within the community of interest while also considering cultural and social factors (Baker, 2001). For this reason, community-based evaluation may be particularly promising for identifying what works to prevent illness and injury in communities disproportionately affected by various health issues, feasible solutions for improving access and decreasing barriers to health care, realistic approaches for increasing skills and knowledge among community members, and innovative ways for disseminating findings to inform future efforts.

Challenges and Solutions for Evaluators

Evaluators interested in addressing racial and ethnic health disparities may enter the field of public health particularly inspired by the notion of actively working with communities to address complex health issues, and impacting sustainable change in the health status of historically underserved minority populations. However, the following sections detail some of the main challenges that evaluators may face and suggested solutions for overcoming these challenges.

Relationships With Community Leaders

Developing and maintaining collaborative partnerships is undoubtedly the foundation of a strong community-based approach. Collaborative partnerships may be developed between researchers and those affected by the health issue of interest, such as individuals who share common space (e.g., urban or rural neighborhood) or experience (e.g., disease diagnosis or living in poverty) (Roussos & Fawcett, 2000). These partnerships can help to create lasting change in the community by identifying realistic solutions for addressing health issues that are specific to the community of interest.

Despite the importance of developing long-lasting relationships within the community, this aspect of community-based research may be especially challenging for evaluators addressing racial and ethnic health disparities. Because of their short time in the field, many evaluators have not yet established meaningful relationships with community leaders or organizations. In addition, there is often a general lack of trust toward health research among minority and disadvantaged groups (Ahmed et al., 2004). As a result,

NEW DIRECTIONS FOR EVALUATION • DOI: 10.1002/ev

many communities are not eager to participate in research or evaluation and may view the research as being manipulative, secretive, and potentially dangerous for them as individuals and the community at large (Ahmed et al., 2004). This lack of trust can be particularly detrimental to evaluators attempting to break into communities.

To overcome this challenge, it is important that evaluators take steps to build trusting relationships in the community that are based on shared decision making, mutual understanding, and respect. Evaluators should have a genuine interest in the community's needs and well-being, and have an ongoing involvement in community activities unrelated to the research in order to build the necessary trust for collaborative partnerships. Evaluators should become part of the community before, during, and after evaluation work takes place in order to truly engage with and understand the community with which they are working.

In addition, evaluators may seek out mentorship from more experienced evaluators utilizing community-based approaches to address racial and ethnic health disparities. Mentors may include academic faculty or senior evaluators with more field experience who can orient the evaluator to the community by introducing them to community leaders and organizations. Evaluators may also identify a community leader to serve as a mentor within the community, someone who can provide additional insight into relationship building within various community settings.

Knowledge of the Community

Many evaluators are armed with a strong foundation in academic knowledge about community-based research principles and evaluation methods. Several academic institutions, as well as private foundations and government agencies, promote and provide education on community-based research and evaluation as a promising approach for addressing complex public health issues. In addition, evaluators bring a fresh perspective to complex research topics and have a wealth of insight to provide to age-old research methods and protocol.

Equally important to an academic background, however, is real-world experience and knowledge of the communities within which new evaluators seek to work. Especially, new evaluators may not have had the opportunity to become intimately knowledgeable about the community, how it operates, how decisions are made, and how lasting changes can be realistically implemented. In addition, evaluators may have a hard to time surrendering some control to the community throughout various phases of the evaluation, as they may feel inclined to stick closely to the rigorous research methods they studied in academic settings.

Similarly to developing collaborative partnerships, evaluators should have a genuine interest in the community and how it functions. Evaluators must take the necessary time to truly consider the community's systems and decision-making processes to ensure that evaluation activities are appropriate in the specific setting. Evaluators should fully utilize community partnerships to inform every step of the evaluation process, from developing grant applications through the dissemination of findings. By utilizing the knowledge and experience of community entities, evaluators can reinforce trusting relationships within the community while improving the credibility and accuracy of their evaluation work.

Resources

It is apparent that conducting community-based research to address racial and ethnic health disparities is a complex undertaking that requires a great deal of effort. Evaluators must devote a great deal of time and effort to develop and maintain the collaborative partnerships that will serve as the foundation for their research. This time commitment may interfere with an evaluator's ability to maintain a consistent work schedule, and she may need to seek support from additional staff to assist in partnership recruitment and development. Additional funding is required to train and compensate these staff to prepare them fully for participation in evaluation work. New evaluators may particularly benefit from providing incentives to communities for participation in evaluation to compensate them for their commitment to the research, reinforce collaborative relationships, and illustrate a genuine appreciation for their contribution.

However, this commitment requires significant resources, particularly funding to support project activities. Evaluators may need to accommodate salary, training, and incentive needs for building partnerships and conducting evaluation. Also, community-based evaluation involves relationship building over time and often requires a longer timeline than clinical research, which may make it difficult for new evaluators to meet grant funding requirements of producing a certain number of publications within a short period of time. Polyani and Cockburn (as cited by Ahmed et al., 2004) also note that the large majority of seed grants offered by academic institutions are for basic, clinical, or educational research, making funding that much more limited and competitive.

Although funding for public health research in general, and community-based evaluation in particular, is limited, evaluators should seek out funding opportunities that allow them to engage communities fully to utilize community-based approaches for addressing racial and ethnic health disparities. Evaluators can explore opportunities to involve volunteers as support staff for the evaluation to alleviate some of the costs. In addition, evaluators may provide communities with intangible incentives for participation, including educational opportunities, access to evaluation data, and technical assistance for intervention implementation and evaluation.

Conclusion

Evaluators committed to addressing racial and ethnic health disparities have innovative ideas to bring to the field of public health evaluation. However, it is imperative that new evaluators are aware of and ready to overcome the unique challenges that new evaluators face when addressing these complex health issues. Coupled with a strong foundational knowledge of community-based approaches and racial and ethnic health disparities, new evaluators are well poised to strengthen the field of public health in overcoming these obstacles.

References

Ahmed, S. M., Beck, B., Maurana, C. A., & Newton, G. (2004). Overcoming barriers to effective community-based participatory research in US medical schools. *Education for Health, 17*(2), 141–151.

Baker, E. (2001). Reducing health disparities through community-based research. *Public Health Reports,* 517–519.

Braveman, P. (2006). Health disparities and health equity: Concepts and measurement. *Annual Review of Public Health,* 167–194.

Centers for Disease Control and Prevention (CDC). (2009). *Eliminating racial and ethnic health disparities.* Retrieved from http://www.cdc.gov/omhd/About/disparities.htm

Giles, W. H., & Liburd, L. C. (2007). Achieving health equity and social justice. In L. Cohen, C. Vivian, & S. Chehimi, *Prevention is primary: Strategies for community well-being* (pp. 25–40). San Francisco, CA: Jossey-Bass.

Roussos, S. T., & Fawcett, S. B. (2000). A review of collaborative partnerships as a strategy for improving community health. *Annual Review of Public Health,* 369–402.

DARA F. SCHLUETER *is a research associate at ICF Macro, a research and consulting firm located in Atlanta, Georgia.*

Robinson, S. B. (2011). Inside, outside, upside down: Challenges and opportunities that frame the future of a novice evaluator. In S. Mathison (Ed.), *Really new directions in evaluation: Young evaluators' perspectives. New Directions for Evaluation, 131*, 65–70.

10

Inside, Outside, Upside Down: Challenges and Opportunities That Frame the Future of a Novice Evaluator

Sheila B. Robinson

Abstract

Through the lens of reflective questions and potential growth opportunities, the author uses as an extended metaphor the popular children's story Inside Outside Upside Down *to illustrate challenges rooted in being a novice evaluator, working inside and outside programs. Given the plethora of evaluation theories and approaches, the author feels "upside down" with decision making, organizing, and prioritizing evaluation projects. How can prominent evaluation theorists' approaches inform a novice evaluator's work and help in developing an identity as an evaluator? Will the author, like the bear in the story, emerge from the box right side up? The author elaborates on how addressing these questions frames how her future as a practicing evaluator might be envisioned.* © Wiley Periodicals, Inc., and the American Evaluation Association.

Inside, Outside, and Upside Down

Going In

Much like others in our field, I too stumbled across evaluation quite by accident and found it a welcome, apropos complement to my education career and graduate studies. As a doctoral student studying educational leadership

I heard the term "program evaluation" in a class. It made sense, of course, that people evaluate programs. But an actual *course* in program evaluation? I was intrigued. What could people study about *evaluation*? Was this a field of inquiry unto itself? By enrolling in the course, and eventually completing the university's evaluation certificate program, I learned the answers and soon found myself drawn inexorably to evaluation. But, much like the unwitting bear in *Inside Outside Upside Down* (Berenstain & Berenstain, 1968) I now find myself in exhilarating yet potentially precarious positions as I undertake evaluation work.

Inside

"You're a program evaluator," my boss said to me. "Can you evaluate our coteaching program (classrooms where general and special educators collaborate to teach integrated groups of students with and without disabilities)?" As a teacher on special assignment, I jumped at the chance to use my evaluation skills. And since I had been both a coteacher and facilitator of coteaching professional development, I understood the program well and mused, "What could be easier?" Ha! A year into the evaluation, including an extensive literature review and attempts to answer the question, "Is it working?" I still don't know whether coteaching is, as my boss originally queried, "making a difference for kids." The challenges appear insurmountable, especially for a novice evaluator. What questions *should* we ask? How can we know if coteaching is making a *difference*? What do we mean by *difference*? What measures can we use? Special education programs and state assessments are rife with complexity and impacted by student transience. How will we account for the vast differences in implementation of coteaching across classrooms and schools?

As an inside evaluator, I am embedded in the program and can barely see the edges. Having lived the program, I am inhibited as an evaluator, empathizing with teachers' distrust of evaluation, and their lack of time to complete surveys or participate in focus groups or interviews. I am less willing to undertake evaluative activities with them, finding the status quo—that is, letting the program continue and evolve without the intrusion of evaluation—somehow more palatable than the seemingly Herculean effort required to empower them to embrace evaluation. It is all I can do to keep my reluctance at bay by honing my evaluation skills, capitalizing on my strengths, and using my role as educator, advocate, *and* evaluator.

Inside a Box

There came one who understood not these things. He said, "Why is this?" Whereupon a million strove to answer him. There was such intricate clamour of tongues, That still the reason was not.

—from *War* by Stephen Crane (Crane & Katz, 1972)

The paradigm wars, that perennial dustup between qualitative and quantitative methodologists—the veritable Hatfields and McCoys of evaluation—loom large for a novice evaluator. How much do methods matter and, ultimately, do I choose them or do they choose me based on the evaluation questions and plan? Patton (2008) admits, ". . . the question of what constitutes *the methodological gold standard* remains hotly contested" (p. 422) and posits, ". . . today's evaluator must be sophisticated about matching research methods to the nuances of particular evaluation questions and the idiosyncrasies of specific decision-maker needs" (p. 466).

Inside a Box Upside Down

Navigating the panoply of evaluation theories and approaches leaves me disoriented and bewildered. All are plausible, tenable, and not beyond the ken of a novice. I am a kid in a candy store: *everything* looks good, all feature common, enticing ingredients, yet the flavors are distinctly different. Still, they will all taste good, so should I choose an approach that is participatory, democratic, utilization-focused, empowering, collaborative, real-world, responsive, goal-driven, or goal-free? How can this startling array of theories and approaches inform my work while developing my own philosophy and identity as an evaluator? What if my approach is determined by the information needs of the client and the nature of the evaluation questions? Is it truly incumbent upon *me* to *choose* an approach, or does the approach emerge from the developing evaluation itself? Is eclecticism the answer? For the novice, there exists a most unfortunate degree of tacit knowledge in evaluation, some perspicacity that escapes my grasp, and an overall dearth of understanding of evaluation in practice. "Overall, the field of evaluation lacks evidence about how evaluators actually use their knowledge, experience, and judgment when deciding how to approach evaluations . . ." (Kundin, 2010). How can I uncover this hidden curriculum?

Going Out

Am I *ready* to be an evaluator? Do I have the right skill set and competencies? Shadish (1998) argues that although evaluation is a practice-based field, to be an evaluator, one must know evaluation theory, that unique knowledge base and discourse that shapes our identity. Patton (2010) refers to "a reservoir of knowledge" (p. 20). My evaluation knowledge may more aptly be described as a mere rain barrel, but it rains evaluation every day as I read, learn, and practice, and I am collecting the drops, thus increasing my stores.

Outside

As an outside evaluator, I find that understanding unfamiliar programs enough to negotiate an evaluation plan and contract, and prioritize evaluation tasks, poses a different set of challenges. Social programs are complex entities often comprised of a multitude of interdependent components. How can I peek inside programs to get a sense of what goes on? How can I develop the necessary rapport, trust, understanding, and acceptance of evaluation to gain access, while still respecting people's time and efforts and my own desire to be unobtrusive? What if I must report negative results?

Going to Town on a Truck Outside Inside a Box Upside Down

Quinn (1996) entitles Chapter 1 of *Deep Change*, "Walking Naked into the Land of Uncertainty." Deep change ". . . requires new ways of thinking and behaving. It is change that is major in scope, discontinuous with the past and generally irreversible. [It] distorts existing patterns of action and involves taking risks" (p. 3). This characterization of change is not unlike the experience of becoming an evaluator. Like many of my evaluation students, I enrolled in my first course with no prior understanding of evaluation. Much of what I read made little sense to me at first. I possessed no familiarity with logic models or theories of change, for example, and it took years of learning and thinking in new and different ways for evaluation logic to settle, solidify, and integrate with prior knowledge and my budding practice to become part and parcel of who I am.

Falling Off

While evaluating a small grant-funded arts program where primary data sources include an audience survey distributed during performances, and an information form, I find I must keep my emotions in check as I collect data. How I *cringe* when the client hands me sheets with key pieces missing. "Oh, sorry about that," he says apologetically, "I guess we forgot to fill in that stuff." How I *bristle* when seeing the survey on which the respondent wrote "coot" (as in "old coot") and drew his own check box for the age question, rather than checking "50 or older!" How I want to *scream* when a smart aleck checked "yes" in the box for "are you a student" and wrote "of life" on the "high school, college, or other" line! How my "teacher voice" just *aches* to address the teen who wrote "Your mom" in the space for "city" and "FU" in the space for "zip code"! Why not just leave it blank if he felt uncomfortable divulging that information? "This is *research*, young man! It's not a joke!" I want to scold him. While I constantly remind my evaluation students that all evaluation is "messy," I struggle with this myself.

Coming Out

I seek continuous learning through evaluation work, reading, and involvement in AEA as I refine my practice and address the questions that mark my

NEW DIRECTIONS FOR EVALUATION • DOI: 10.1002/ev

nascent evaluation career. My reading includes journals and university library searches for relevant books and articles. Visits to the AEA e-library, and participation in Coffee Break webinars, *EvalTalk*, and *AEA365 A Tip-a-Day by and for Evaluators* are part of my daily routine. I presented at Evaluation 2010, connected with several topical interest groups, and joined the leadership of one. I now collaborate with like-minded evaluators nationwide who are proving a tremendous source of learning and support.

I seek mentors in the field—former classmates, professors, and colleagues. And, I look to the rock stars of evaluation, whose prolific writing substantially adds to my knowledge base and my understanding of the unique discourse of evaluation, and ultimately informs my practice. My Mick Jagger of evaluation is Michael Quinn Patton, whose work on utilization-focused and developmental evaluation holds particular appeal for me, not only for its content and focus, but for Patton's inimitable cogent-yet-humorous, delicate-yet-deliberate, academic-yet-conversational style.

Right Side Up!

What do I value in evaluation? What kind of evaluator am I? Where might I be on Alkin and Christie's (2004) evaluation theory tree, that well-known conceptual map of individuals whose work has significantly contributed to this field? In studying the names on the tree, I find I admire and use individuals' work from all three branches: use, methods, and valuing. I am hopeful that my future as a practicing evaluator and contributor to this inspiring field holds promise, and I look forward to learning more from veteran evaluators and researchers about the nature of evaluation in practice. I hope they help me bridge the theory–practice gap, gain a fresh perspective in evaluative thinking, and finally locate myself in this dynamic field.

Mama! Mama! I Went to Town. Inside, Outside, Upside Down!

Patton (2010), in discussing developmental evaluation, likens complexity to hiking the Grand Canyon, but this metaphor aptly illustrates the experiences of a novice evaluator.

> . . . sidetracks. Unexpected detours. Getting lost. Navigating through rough terrain. Negotiating ravines and ridges. Steep ascents and terrifying descents. Diverging, converging, and crisscrossing. Watching for what emerges. Expecting the unexpected. Going with the flow. Riding cascades and waves of turbulence. (p. 8)

As an avid hiker, I can relate. Like evaluation work, it certainly is difficult, but well worth the trip. And lest I become overwhelmed with questions as I develop my praxis, I take comfort in these words: "There is no one best way to conduct evaluation" (Patton, 2010, p. 15).

NEW DIRECTIONS FOR EVALUATION • DOI: 10.1002/ev

References

Alkin, M. C., & Christie, C. A. (2004). An evaluation theory tree. In M. C. Alkin (Ed.), *Evaluation roots: Tracing theorists' views and influences* (pp. 12–65). Thousand Oaks, CA: Sage.

Berenstain, S., & Berenstain, J. (1968). *Inside outside upside down.* New York, NY: Random House.

Crane, S., & Katz, J. (1972). *The complete poems of Stephen Crane.* Ithaca, NY: Cornell University Press.

Kundin, D. M. (2010). A conceptual framework for how evaluators make everyday practice decisions. *American Journal of Evaluation, 31*(3), 347–362.

Patton, M. Q. (2008). *Utilization-focused evaluation* (4th ed.). Los Angeles, CA: Sage.

Patton, M. Q. (2010). *Developmental evaluation: Applying complexity concepts to enhance innovation and use.* New York, NY: Guilford Press.

Quinn, R. E. (1996). *Deep change: Discovering the leader within.* San Francisco, CA: Jossey-Bass.

Shadish, W. R. (1998). Evaluation theory is who we are. *American Journal of Evaluation, 19*(1), 1–19.

SHEILA B. ROBINSON is an adjunct professor at the University of Rochester's Warner School of Education and a teacher on special assignment for the Greece Central School District in Rochester, NY.

White, P., & Boulton, A. (2011). Sailing through relationships? On discovering the compass for navigating 21st-century evaluation in the Pacific. In S. Mathison (Ed.), *Really new directions in evaluation: Young evaluators' perspectives. New Directions for Evaluation, 131*, 71–76.

11

Sailing Through Relationships? On Discovering the Compass for Navigating 21st-Century Evaluation in the Pacific

Paula White, Amohia Boulton

Abstract

Aotearoa New Zealand is a small bicultural island nation in the Pacific with a multicultural population, a context that poses unique challenges for new evaluators, as it does for our more experienced counterparts. As emerging evaluators, the key challenge we have faced is navigating relationships, at the interface between program funders and culturally diverse communities, with integrity, and to ensure meaningful, credible, and valid evaluation findings. Drawing on their early experiences, the authors discuss their discoveries on sailing through relationships toward evaluation that is "good." © Wiley Periodicals, Inc., and the American Evaluation Association.

E kore e ngaro, he takere waka nui

The hull of a canoe cannot be lost (Mead & Grove, 1989)[1]

At the dawn of the 21st century, we have come to understand as emerging evaluators how much relationships matter to our work—theoretically, conceptually, and practically. We elaborate on this point in our article, drawing an analogy with the ancient Pacific navigators, who built craft and sailed across long stretches of open sea, using the knowledge, techniques, and collective wisdom available to them—of landmarks, currents, and tides, the sun and the stars. We reveal our main discovery that navigating relationships well is like a compass for reaching good evaluation. We identify some specific challenges that have surfaced for us in our unique evaluation context, and highlight the opportunities they present for landing our craft safely on future evaluation shores.

Aotearoa New Zealand, the shores we call home, is today a predominantly Pākehā (non-Māori) society, with a democratically elected Westminster-style government. Our small population of some four million people comprises diverse peoples including Māori (the indigenous peoples), those with European heritage, Pacific Island peoples, and many newer immigrants from other continents. When Māori and the British Crown signed the Treaty of Waitangi in 1840, Māori enshrined in it their rights to live as Māori, and this is regarded by many as our country's founding document (Te Puni Kōkiri, 2001). Importantly, the Treaty outlined a relationship by which the indigenous peoples and colonial settlers would coexist. In 2011, the Treaty serves as a landmark for us, a reference point for new evaluators embarking on evaluation.

Departure Points: Two Emerging Evaluators in Aotearoa New Zealand

Notwithstanding our different backgrounds and work contexts, we share a parallel current focus on Māori evaluation in the social sector specifically. We work at the interface of similar evaluation stakeholders, largely because in our country the majority of social-sector programs are funded publicly through central government, and delivered by nongovernment community providers. We have each developed our evaluation capability through formal academic training, through learning from the wisdom of colleagues and mentors, and through our experiences (and mistakes) applying that wisdom. We have learned that in developing our evaluation expertise, theoretical literature, training, and checklists are all helpful, but there is no substitute for the experiential knowledge we have gained through practice. There is an element of sink or swim for new evaluators here, and we have observed a pragmatic undercurrent in local evaluation, one drawing from a strong pragmatic action research tradition (Williams, 2007). In Māori evaluation specifically, the desire of Māori evaluators to work in a participatory way—to upskill those who are the focus of evaluation, to build community capacity, and to advance local community development objectives—is reflective of broader currents in the social sciences here.

Turning Tides: Broad Influences on the Direction of Our Craft

Since the 1970s Māori academics made significant efforts to reframe Māori research; redirecting it away from being a tool to describe Māori society, to being a vehicle by which Māori could reclaim their own theoretical and methodological perspectives (Smith, 1999). This reclamation process involved deep consideration about who should undertake research with Māori (Stokes, 1992), what the ethical considerations are when researching with Māori (Cram, 1995), and what Māori communities might expect of research (Durie, 1992). A direct consequence of this reflection was the renaissance of Kaupapa Māori (Māori-centered) approaches to research and evaluation.

Today many government-funded social programs in our country aim to redress the impact of colonization on Māori and political, cultural, and social inequities that have resulted from our nation's history. Evaluations of such programs by Māori practitioners are characterized by a strong commitment to identifying the ways in which programs are addressing those inequities. Moreover, there is a strong sense that all evaluations relating to and undertaken by or for Māori must serve Māori and positively contribute to the communities in which we live, as well as inform government policy and decision making (Wehipeihana, 2008). As Kaupapa Māori approaches have become more visible, Pākehā research and evaluation counterparts have been challenged to reflect on the meaning of ethical practice in our bicultural setting, on notions of cross-cultural safety (Ramsden, 2002), and on meaningful cross-cultural engagement.

Finding Our Compass: Staying On Course Through Relationships

Our evaluation training highlighted the generic importance of brokering relationships in evaluation, yet in our unique national context this task can be likened to navigating high seas—with hazards that have thrown us into the water unexpectedly, or grounded us. In fact, evaluation in Aotearoa New Zealand sometimes feels like paddling in a shallow lagoon, one in which all evaluation stakeholders (past, present, and future) are highly visible to us—and us to them. What has helped us most to manage this complex relationship environment successfully has been our own professional relationships within the evaluation community. We have both ensured we remain connected with professional evaluation networks and taken advantage of professional learning opportunities. More importantly perhaps, we have both sought out experienced evaluation mentors who have sailed through these waters before us and whose advice has often helped light the way forward.

In our country, new and experienced evaluators alike must navigate successfully across, and within, different cultures and norms in the diverse communities in which we live. We have learned that maintaining relationship integrity in evaluation is key and our experiences confirm that this task is not straightforward. Garnering the trust of each evaluation stakeholder—whether evaluation commissioner, program staff, or community representative—from the outset of any evaluation, and maintaining the level of comfort of all evaluation stakeholders throughout the course of the evaluation, is a delicate balancing act that can test even the steadiest of craft. Simply applying advanced Western evaluation approaches here may fail to recognize the holistic and relational cultural norms of some communities, and this will be problematic for those aiming for meaningful evaluation findings that reflect evaluation-participant perceptions of what is valid and credible (Newport, 2003).

In Māori evaluation specifically, the role of whakapapa (ancestry and family and community family ties), trust, and long-term reciprocal relationships that are integral to tikanga Māori (Māori practice and values) are critical (Moewaka Barnes, 2009), as much so as international evaluation theory about good practice. Amohia explains:

> As a Māori person, undertaking evaluation with Māori, my role and my responsibilities are governed by tikanga Māori as well as good evaluation and research practice from a "Western" point of view. In consulting with potential evaluation participants, I clarify my expectations at the outset, as well as what participants might expect from me. My accountability to evaluation participants and to the Māori community more widely is always discussed. Establishing a relationship of trust early on is crucial, and the ethical obligation uppermost in my mind throughout the evaluation is to contribute in a positive manner to Māori aspirations for their own development. Remaining true to this obligation requires a significant time commitment; however the rewards, in terms of the richness of the data and the relationships that are forged, cannot be underestimated.

Nonetheless, we have observed colleagues adapting international evaluation concepts here with some success. For example, Conner's (2010) "Draw the Path" technique and Patton's (2011) "Developmental Evaluation" both appear to have a resonance with the important relational dimensions of Aotearoa New Zealand evaluation practice.

We have discovered that our own self-knowledge and cultural capital informs our choice of evaluation approach and our processes of engagement with stakeholders. Our experiences testify to the idea that evaluation is as much about who we are as evaluators, and where we position ourselves in relation to others in our work, as it is about what we do and how we do it (Greene, 2005). Precisely because our lagoon is so small, we must ensure our evaluation practice is above reproach. The integrity we bring to our work is critical to ensure that our evaluation participants and the communities we impact are not harmed, and yet our personal responsibility goes beyond this. We think our evaluation practice should uphold the trust placed in us, should enhance the mana (integrity) of the people and communities we work with, and should contribute to social transformation

(Mertens, 2009). We know that our evaluation peers, participants, and beneficiaries are evaluating us too—the ultimate performance indicator for whether we attain evaluation that is "good."

Making New Waves: Toward Evaluation as Social Navigation

The most significant challenges we have faced in the evaluation of social programs in Aotearoa New Zealand relate to the skillful navigation of relationships. We have discovered that building effective relationships and trust with evaluation commissioners, participants, and beneficiaries across and within diverse cultures provides real opportunities for evaluation success. Navigating these relationships is not easy, and we must know and articulate who we are and the value we bring to evaluation, and seek understanding and brokerage of the values of all evaluation stakeholders. In particular, our ability to forge and maintain trust with evaluation stakeholders is like a compass bearing for the credibility, validity, and impact of our evaluation results. We can see this both in the waves we are making and in the wakes of more experienced local and international counterparts. We will continue to measure the "goodness" of our evaluation practice by how well we navigate relationships to make a positive contribution to our fellow human beings. In maintaining such a robust hull in our practice, we hope to stay on the right course in our continuing evaluation journeys.

Note

1. In contemporary times this Māori proverb can mean that if an institution such as a family is strong, it can withstand many temporary setbacks.

References

Conner, R. (2010). *Draw the path: A technique for evaluation and planning.* [Powerpoint slides]. Auckland, New Zealand.

Cram, F. (1995). *Ethics and cross cultural research.* Auckland, New Zealand: University of Auckland, Department of Psychology.

Durie, A. (1992). *Whaia te ara tika: Research methodologies and Māori* (seminar on Māori research). Palmerston North, New Zealand: Massey University.

Greene, J. C. (2005). Evaluators as stewards of the public good. In S. Hood, R. Hopson, & H. Frierson (Eds.), *The role of culture and cultural context: A mandate for inclusion, the discovery of truth and understanding in evaluative theory and practice* (pp. 7–20). Charlotte, NC: Information Age.

Mead, H. M., & Grove, N. (1989). *The sayings of the ancestors.* Wellington, New Zealand: Victoria University Press.

Mertens, D. M. (2009). *Transformative research and evaluation.* New York, NY: Guilford Press.

Moewaka Barnes, H. M. (2009). *The evaluation hikoi: A Māori overview of programme evaluation.* Auckland, New Zealand: Massey University Te Rōpū Whāriki.

Newport, C. (2003). Pacific evaluation: Values, voices and methodological considerations. In N. Lunt, C. Davidson, & K. McKegg (Eds.), *Evaluating policy and practice. A New Zealand reader* (pp. 236–239). Auckland, New Zealand: Pearson Education.

Patton, M. Q. (2011). *Developmental evaluation. Applying complexity concepts to enhance innovation and use.* New York, NY: Guilford Press.

Ramsden, I. (2002). *Cultural safety and nursing education in Aotearoa and Te Waipounamu* (Unpublished doctoral dissertation). Victoria University of Wellington, Wellington, New Zealand.

Smith, L. T. (1999). *Decolonizing methodologies. Research and indigenous peoples* (8th ed.). Dunedin, New Zealand: University of Otago Press.

Stokes, E. (1992). Māori research and development: A discussion paper. In M. Hohepa & G. H. Smith, *The issue of research and Maori monograph.* Auckland, New Zealand: University of Auckland.

Te Puni Kōkiri. (2001). *He Tirohanga o Kawa ki te Tiriti o Waitangi.* Wellington, New Zealand: Te Puni Kōkiri.

Wehipeihana, N. (2008). Indigenous evaluation. A strategic objective of the Australasian Evaluation Society. *Evaluation Journal of Australasia, 8*(1), 40–44.

Williams, B. (2007, November 2). Bridging real gaps in evaluation [Msg 2]. Message posted to American Evaluation Association Discussion electronic mailing list, archived at http://bama.ua.edu/cgi-bin/wa?A1=ind0711a&L=evaltalk&X=43E6EE3B7DFA 22B178#4.

PAULA WHITE *is a Senior Advisor Evaluation with Te Puni Kōkiri, the Ministry of Māori Development in Wellington, New Zealand; she was formerly a monitoring and evaluation consultant and a Senior Monitoring and Evaluation Advisor at Sport and Recreation New Zealand.*

AMOHIA BOULTON *(Ngāti Ranginui, Ngai te Rangi, and Ngāti Pukenga) is a Senior Researcher at Whakauae Research in Whanganui, New Zealand, and holds the position of visiting senior research fellow at the Health Services Research Centre, School of Government, Victoria University, Wellington.*

NEW DIRECTIONS FOR EVALUATION • DOI: 10.1002/ev

Baxter, C. E. (2011). Integrating a new evaluation unit with an old institution: See no evil; hear no evil; speak no evil. In S. Mathison (Ed.), *Really new directions in evaluation: Young evaluators' perspectives. New Directions for Evaluation, 131*, 77–81.

12

Integrating a New Evaluation Unit With an Old Institution: See No Evil; Hear No Evil; Speak No Evil

Claire E. Baxter

Abstract

The author focuses on issues related to the implementation and acceptance of a new evaluation unit within an organization. Specifically, the author discusses role clarity of the evaluation unit with respect to overlapping roles and the reach of the evaluation unit. The author also discusses the push-and-pull relationship between organization and evaluation staff. © Wiley Periodicals, Inc., and the American Evaluation Association.

The recent push for organizations and institutions to demonstrate more accountability and program efficacy, especially in today's economy, has moved the practice of evaluation to the forefront of organizations and institutions. Thus, new evaluation units are emerging in organizations and institutions where evaluation may be unfamiliar to many members of the organization. Careful planning and consideration is needed to ensure that the evaluation unit is visible and seen as a beneficial unit of the organization.

The author would like to thank Anne Bergen and Alayna Panzer for feedback on an earlier draft.

NEW DIRECTIONS FOR EVALUATION, no. 131, Fall 2011   © Wiley Periodicals, Inc., and the American Evaluation Association.   Published online in Wiley Online Library (wileyonlinelibrary.com) • DOI: 10.1002/ev.382

I will discuss issues that I have noted recently as a newcomer to evaluation, as a doctoral student in applied social psychology with a focus on program evaluation. My evaluation experience includes evaluation framework and logic model development, needs assessments, outcome evaluations, and organizational performance measurement. I have worked as a graduate practicum student, a consultant in the social-service sector, and currently, as a research assistant in an evaluation unit at an academic library. Through these experiences, I have been able to observe and compare how organizations handle their evaluations across a number of different settings. In this article, I will discuss issues related to the integration of new evaluation units such as the role and purpose of these units and the pushback associated with evaluation efforts.

Role Clarity

There is a sizeable literature on the evolution of the evaluation unit and the many issues experienced by internal evaluators (Love, 1991; Mathison, 1991a, 1991b, 1994; Sonnichsen, 2000). Specifically, role conflicts faced by the professional evaluator operating as a member of an organization and a substantive community have been discussed (Mathison, 1991a, 1991b), and, most recently, issues faced implementing the evaluation unit in a political environment have been noted (Chelimsky, 2009). The majority of the extant literature discusses issues faced by the evaluator or the evaluation unit and, though not entirely distinct, I will take the perspective of organizational staff and discuss the barriers they face (or sometimes put in place) in identifying the role of the evaluation unit and accessing its services. Specifically, there are two main issues regarding role confusion that occur: (a) overlapping organizational units, and (b) issues related to the reach of the evaluation unit.

Overlapping Units

Sonnichsen (2000) describes the evaluation unit (from the perspective of organizational staff) as ambiguous and an enigma, and attributes an ambiguous reputation of an evaluation unit, in part, to an "ill-defined and largely misunderstood mission" (p. 265). I believe that a clearly defined mission is of premier importance within a larger organization, where there is a greater chance that two units may serve a similar purpose. In my experience, I have noticed that in larger institutions, there are overlapping research and evaluation departments that serve the same staff members. For example, I work in an evaluation unit within an academic library. We conduct large-scale internal evaluations and help to facilitate organizational staff conduct their own evaluations by providing guidance with data collection and analysis. Within the library there is also a data resource center that holds statistical/numerical and geospatial data collections, but also provides support in the use of these types of data. In addition, the greater university offers a research office that houses the research ethics review board, a psychology department that teaches program evaluation, and a mathematics and statistics department that offers statistical consultants. As an evaluation staff member, it is clear to me (one year in) what types of services we offer and to whom, but through a number of formal and informal interactions, I have realized that these distinctions are not as clear to others and I do not believe this to be a unique situation. Previously, I worked as a research intern in an evaluation unit at a mental health research hospital that evaluated external community programs, but the unit was not responsible for internal evaluation. In addition, there was a research operations department that provided research methods guidance and helped to facilitate research activities in other departments. I assume that each clinical department was responsible for their own program evaluations. However, if someone had a question regarding evaluation methodology, it was unclear to me whether they would consult the evaluation unit or whether they would contact the research operations department, who may or may not have expertise in evaluation.

It is already known that in order to prevent this type of confusion, a clearly defined mission is vital and this mission needs to be clearly communicated and marketed to all organizational staff (Sonnichsen, 2000). Cross-communication between departments that share a similar role will increase awareness of their services, and assist in clarifying the boundaries of their services as well as the identification of their unique role. I believe it would also decrease the extent to which organizational staff get lost in the system, as cross-communication will likely increase more accurate referrals between departments. I believe that an institution can accommodate these types of overlap, but in order for the organizational structure to work, these distinctions need to be clearly mapped out and effectively communicated.

The Reach of the Evaluation Unit

In our evaluation unit at the library, our organizational structure resembles a combination of both a centralized and decentralized evaluation unit. We are a separate and independent unit and report to upper management; however, because the existing library departments were already conducting their own research and evaluation before the implementation of our evaluation unit, we help them to facilitate their own evaluations. This approach helps us to gain the advantages of a centralized unit, such that we have greater evaluative independence, an ability to create an institutional evaluation memory, and a direct line to upper management (Sonnichsen, 2000). It also helps us to gain an advantage of a decentralized unit, such that we have reduced the evaluation threat often felt towards the centralized evaluation unit (Sonnichsen, 2000). However, this structure makes our role a bit fuzzy. Because there is research being conducted in many forms and in every department, from haphazard to systematic evaluations, general system counts, and personal research conducted by librarians, it is not always clear what types of research we should be involved in and where our role begins and ends. This abundance of data collection and analysis presents a number of issues for our evaluation unit. For example, librarians are encouraged to conduct their own personal research for tenure purposes. Mandating our evaluation unit to be involved in all aspects of their research would not be particularly ideal, as their position entitles them to a degree of academic freedom and their research may not be evaluation based. However, they can ask for research methods or data-analysis help. For this reason, it then becomes difficult for evaluation staff and internal staff to understand where the line is drawn. Again, a clearly defined role that is clearly communicated would certainly help ease organizational interactions with, in this case, our evaluation unit; however, I believe that a clearly defined role will only help if it is understandable to organizational staff. It is quite possible that a librarian might understand evaluation as solely outcome evaluation and not realize that the research he or she is conducting is a needs assessment that falls under the evaluation unit's responsibility and may not think to ask for help. The role of the evaluation unit should be described in plain language with a limit on evaluation jargon, so that the activities of the evaluation unit are not a mystery and are accessible by all.

Push and Pull

The final important issue that I have encountered as an evaluator is in marketing evaluation. In general, evaluation units are not the authority through which all evaluation research must be approved, as is the case for research and research ethics review boards. Evaluation can be conducted in any organizational unit without the involvement of the evaluation unit staff. The extent to which this is discouraged depends on the initial framework of the unit and the organizational structure. In our case, we facilitate evaluation activities in other departments, but without a mandate from upper management a program manager can decide not to participate and the evaluation does not occur. As there is no strict policy or penalty for not collaborating, we have no authority to ensure participation in evaluation. The difficulty in receiving buy-in for evaluation activities is not a new concept (Patton, 1997), but it seems to be amplified when there is an absence of a mandate from upper management. Resistance to evaluation stems from a number of reasons including the fear of statistics, inconvenience, and fear of failure (Patton, 1997; Sonnichsen, 2000). This lack of authority and resistance results in passive pushback in the form of unanswered phone calls (hear no evil), unanswered emails (see no evil), and no-shows at meetings (speak no evil).

To address this problem our evaluation unit has developed an evaluation and assessment committee, which includes a staff member representative from each department. Terms of reference were developed that help to increase accountability. This committee provided a means for us to teach and implement performance-measuring strategies and logic modeling in each unit. With the use of a train-the-trainer approach, the committee members were asked to disseminate their learning to their own departments and to attempt to develop logic models and performance measures with their colleagues for their unit's programs. To date, it has been successful in helping to increase the awareness of our evaluation services and expertise. It provides a forum for open communication where they can gain feedback, not solely from us, but from other committee members. Most importantly, it has helped to produce champions of evaluation in each library department. We anticipate that this will help to assuage the evaluation resistance from some units and will provide a representative to speak to if collaboration problems are encountered. Overall, the formation of this committee has helped to bring forward systematic evaluation, maybe not to the forefront just yet, but to a satisfying middle ground.

Final Thoughts

With the steady increase in accountability pressures in every type of organization and industry, evaluation units are here to stay. Thus, it is important that careful consideration is provided in the initial integration phase of the evaluation unit so that it is accepted as a valuable component of the organization. It is essential that the unit's role is clearly mapped out in relation to the existing organizational structure and is clearly communicated to all staff and clients. Overall, in my experience as a newcomer to evaluation, I believe that attention to these issues will result in a smoother integration of new evaluation units into older and more established institutions.

References

Chelimsky, E. (2009). Integrating evaluation units into the political environment of government: The role of evaluation policy. In W. M. K. Trochim, M. M. Mark, & L. J. Cooksy (Eds.), *Evaluation policy and evaluation practice. New Directions for Evaluation, 123,* 51–66.

Love, A. (1991). *Internal evaluation: Building organizations from within.* Newbury Park, CA: Sage.

Mathison, S. (1991a). What do we know about internal evaluation? *Evaluation and Program Planning, 14,* 159–165.

Mathison, S. (1991b). Role conflicts for internal evaluators. *Evaluation and Program Planning, 14,* 173–179.

Mathison, S. (1994). Rethinking the evaluator role: Partnerships between organizations and evaluators. *Evaluation and Program Planning, 17*(3), 299–304.

Patton, M. Q. (1997). *Utilization-focused evaluation* (3rd ed.). Thousand Oaks, CA: Sage.

Sonnichsen, R. C. (2000). *High impact internal evaluation.* Thousand Oaks, CA: Sage.

CLAIRE E. BAXTER IS a doctoral student in the Department of Psychology and an evaluation research assistant at the University of Guelph.

Derrick-Mills, T. M. (2011). Building the value of evaluation: Engaging with reflective practitioners. In S. Mathison (Ed.), *Really new directions in evaluation: Young evaluators' perspectives. New Directions for Evaluation, 131,* 83–90.

13

Building the Value of Evaluation: Engaging With Reflective Practitioners

Teresa M. Derrick-Mills

Abstract

*Evaluation use has been a focal point of the evaluation field for many years, and
recent practice and theory have focused on the potentially transformative effects
of the evaluation process itself. All of these efforts, however, start with practitioners who are frequently fearful or suspicious about the process mandated or
imposed on them, concerned about the time it will take away from their direct
service, and dubious of the value that the evaluation will impart. Although the
efforts of individual evaluators attempting to partner with practitioners one program at a time to improve the evaluation process and convince practitioners of
its value are important, we also need systemic approaches to cultivate the value
of evaluation among practitioners. This chapter proposes a three-pronged
approach to develop and engage reflective practitioners to build the value of evaluation.* © Wiley Periodicals, Inc., and the American Evaluation Association.

On September 28, 2010, Laura Leviton posed the question, "How can
we learn from communities of practice?" as the title of her post to
the American Evaluation Association's (AEA's) Thought Leader's
Forum. In this post and others that followed, Leviton discussed the possible
contributions of reflective practitioners in communities of practice to
improving understanding of the external validity of evaluations. Leviton uses
Cronbach's UTOS (that is, units, treatments, observations, settings) to

describe how and where reflective practitioners may be helpful to evaluators. She identifies the reflective practitioner as being helpful in the development and testing of programs where "reflective practitioners in particular . . . will best assist [evaluators] with sharper operationalization of treatments and extrapolation to *UTOS," and in better identifying "the dimensions of the sampling frame for *UTOS that are worth studying, for the best probes and tests of external validity" (Leviton, 2010). Leviton frequently emphasizes, however, that her point is not about the engagement of a single reflective practitioner here and there, but rather about a systematic engagement of many reflective practitioners with a high volume of practitioner experience.

Where do we find these reflective practitioners and how does the evaluation community engage with them? In this article I propose a three-pronged approach for the evaluation community to engage systematically with reflective practitioners and build the value of evaluation in doing so. The evaluation community should (1) help to develop reflective practitioners by encouraging the inclusion of evaluation coursework as a mandatory component of relevant degree programs, (2) regularly engage with reflective practitioners at their professional development gatherings, and (3) build upon the platform that mandatory performance measurement creates in government and nonprofit organizations. Before explicating each of these approaches, I provide some context, and then I provide suggestions for further research.

The Current Environment

Given that program evaluation has been prominent at the federal level since the 1960s and that the reinventing government movement heralded in performance measures for federal, state, and local governments, and nonprofit organizations in the 1990s, we might be lulled into thinking that programs billed as educating the future government and nonprofit workforce regularly include program evaluation as a standard part of their curriculum. A review of the 142 websites of NASPAA-accredited Master of Public Administration/Public Affairs programs, however, indicates otherwise. Only 29% (37 of 129 programs with sufficient information on their websites) require a core course where the title contains *evaluation* (retrieved March 5–6, 2011).

An examination of the NASPAA Commission on Peer Review & Accreditation 2010–2011 Roster of Accredited Programs shows there are 142 Master of Public Administration/Public Affairs programs. A review of the websites of each program was conducted, looking for on-line information indicating whether a core course with the word *evaluation* in the title appeared. Thirteen websites did not provide enough on-line information to determine if a course with *evaluation* in the title was part of the core curriculum; 37 programs had such a core course; 11 additional programs included it as part of their extended core courses; 81 programs did not include it as any kind of core course. Although programs accredited by the National Association of Public Affairs and Administration (NASPAA) are clearly a subset of schools offering degrees in public administration and public affairs, this cursory assessment indicates there is reason to be concerned.

Building the Value of Evaluation

The three-pronged approach that I propose for building the value of evaluation calls for the evaluation community, the institutions that define and embody program evaluation, to develop and engage with reflective practitioners systematically. The intermediate goal of this approach is to increase the value of evaluation, that is, to help practitioners understand why evaluation could be meaningful for them and their programs, and to better inform program evaluations. Ultimately, the goal is to help the evaluation community and the practitioner community to be engaged together routinely to create informed, effective, efficient public programs ameliorating long-term societal problems.

The proposed approaches recognize that the evaluation community continuously works to provide its members with opportunities to improve their professional development, including how to relate to practitioners. It also acknowledges that individual evaluators may systematically engage practitioners during each evaluation they perform. The proposed approaches do not negate the value of these efforts, but rather they suggest a supplement to existing efforts.

1. The evaluation community should help to develop reflective practitioners by encouraging the inclusion of evaluation coursework as a mandatory component of relevant degree programs.

Although the Master of Public Administration/Public Affairs (MPA) is not the only degree that practitioners working in governments or nonprofit organizations may hold, it is touted by the National Association of Schools of Public Administration and Affairs (NASPAA) as "preparing students to be leaders, managers, and analysts in the professions of public affairs, public administration, and public policy" (NASPAA Commission on Peer Review & Accreditation, 2009, p. 2). According to NASPAA, it only accredits programs where public-service values are imbued in the curriculum: "They include pursuing the public interest with accountability and transparency; serving professionally with competence, efficiency, and objectivity; acting ethically so as to uphold the public trust; and demonstrating respect, equity, and fairness in dealings with citizens and fellow public servants" (NASPAA Commission on Peer Review & Accreditation, 2009, p. 2). Clearly these standards do not preclude the inclusion of program evaluation as part of the core curriculum, but what is the message sent by the small

NEW DIRECTIONS FOR EVALUATION • DOI: 10.1002/ev

number of MPA programs requiring program evaluation? The message is that program evaluation is optional, not just in a public servant's education, but also in the practice of public administration. If it isn't a required course, then it must not be a necessary part of public service.

If the evaluation community believes that program evaluation is an essential part of public service and its execution differs from other research methods traditionally taught in MPA programs, then it needs to make clear the unique value that program evaluation contributes to public-service values. In addition, the evaluation community needs to determine what other degree programs frequently yield public service managers, and to investigate and engage with those programs to encourage the inclusion of program evaluation coursework.

2. The evaluation community should regularly engage with reflective practitioners at their professional development gatherings.

Once practitioners finish their initial degrees, they remain informed of what is important to their field through memberships in professional associations and attendance at professional development events such as conferences. Program evaluation likely has natural ambassadors, because many program evaluators have degrees in other fields or they naturally situate their work in a particular content area, like health, education, the environment, and so on. The evaluation community, however, should strategically target professions where they would like to develop reflective practitioners, recruit ambassadors to attend relevant professional development gatherings, and provide the ambassadors with the tools they need to help educate and engage with the practitioners. It is important to send ambassadors who speak both the language of evaluation and the language of the practitioners to build bridges to share knowledge.

3. The evaluation community should build upon the platform that mandatory performance measurement creates in government and non-profit organizations.

Although there is not agreement on whether performance measurement and performance management are the best strategies for improving programs, it is, in fact, the case that governments and funders frequently require them. Given that this is the environment in which practitioners exist, the evaluation community should help practitioners transform the process: "Translating performance measurement exercises into organizational learning about program theory requires that managers think like evaluators, and such thinking needs to be groomed and supported" (Newcomer, 2001, p. 339).

Because most managers (practitioners) are not trained to think like evaluators, they may not understand how to translate their knowledge into performance measurement despite requirements to do so. Without the involvement of evaluators, these well-intentioned practitioners may lose out on both avenues for their own learning and avenues to shape future program evaluations. Patton (2008) describes the relationship between performance measurement and program evaluation this way:

> [Performance] Indicators tell us whether something is increasing, declining, or staying the same. Evaluation takes us deeper into asking why indicators are moving in the direction they are, how the movement of indicators are related to specific interventions, what is driving the movement of indicators, and what values should guide interpretation of indicators in making judgments. (pp. 258–259)

Wholey (1986, 1996, 2001) similarly advocates for evaluators to help agencies craft performance measures and performance measurement systems. Drawing inspiration from the exhortations of Wholey, comments made by Hatry, Newcomer, Poister, and Henry (Strengthening Evaluation Effectiveness, 2011), and posts made by Leviton (2010) as she hosted the AEA Thought Leader's Forum, I depict the symbiotic relationship between performance measurement and evaluation in Figure 13.1. The top row of the figure represents any typical performance measurement system. The cross (*agency regularly analyzes PM data*) represents a crossroads where the symbiosis creates value in three ways:

1. The analysis can be used directly to improve the program (Hatry, Morely, Rossman, & Wholey, 2005; Moynihan, 2007; Poister, 2004; Wholey, 2001).
2. The analysis can generate "how" and "why" questions that require a program evaluation for answers (Wholey, 1986, 1996, 2001).
3. The analysis can yield information that improves program evaluation design options (Strengthening Evaluation Effectiveness, 2011) and understanding of external validity (Leviton, 2010).

The dotted lines represent processes that have the potential to improve programs or improve evaluation research, but this potential is likely to be realized only where reflective practitioners and evaluators have engaged in the process together.

In reflection with practitioners, the evaluator can help the practitioner to focus his or her attention, create organizational learning, and generate new information about the program. If the evaluator participates on the front end, he or she will have built an important relationship with the practitioner before an evaluation happens, and will have laid the groundwork for important data to inform the eventual evaluation.

Figure 13.1. The Symbiotic Relationship Between Performance Measurement (PM) and Evaluation

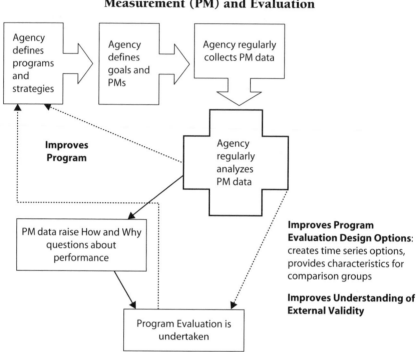

Conclusion and Suggestions for Future Research

This article was inspired in part by Leviton's (2010) question "How can we learn from communities of practice?" I have proposed an answer to the question, but I view this answer as the beginning of a conversation, not the end. In addition, Leviton's question is multidimensional, and I have addressed only one aspect of it here. I hope as a field that we will more fully explore it together.

If the evaluation field were to accept the approaches I have proposed, we should evaluate our efforts to build the value of evaluation. We should document our starting place and the progress we make, and attempt to understand the ultimate contribution of our efforts. One such strategy is suggested by Patrizi's (2010) generic evaluation framework for tracking strategies. Thus, I offer these preliminary suggestions for future research regarding the three-pronged approach discussed here for improving the value of evaluation.

1. Create a formal inventory of evaluation coursework offered in graduate programs that typically produce public service managers.

A formal inventory now will create a baseline for measuring the effect of efforts to increase the inclusion of evaluation. Understanding the current offerings can help craft outreach strategies to accrediting bodies, schools, and professional associations. (Note that this is different from the list of schools currently available on AEA's website that offer a concentration in program evaluation.)

2. Study efforts to realize the potential symbiosis between performance measurement and evaluation efforts.

Does research confirm that efforts to create the symbiosis correlate with more use of performance measures and/or evaluation to inform programs? Do efforts to facilitate the symbiosis result in improved understanding of external validity? Do efforts to facilitate the symbiosis result in differing evaluation approaches?

3. What can we learn about our efforts to engage with the practitioner community?

What strategy dimensions worked the best? Where were there gaps in our strategy? How did we adapt and how can we apply what we learned in the future?

References

Hatry, H. P., Morely, E., Rossman, S. B., & Wholey, J. S. (2005). How federal programs use outcome information: Opportunities for federal managers. In J. M. Kamensky & A. Morales (Eds.), for the IBM Center for the Business of Government, *Managing for results 2005* (pp. 197–274). Lanham, MD: Rowman & Littlefield.

Leviton, L. (2010, October). AEA Thought Leader's Forum. Retrieved from http://comm.eval.org/EVAL/EVAL/Discussions/ViewThread/Default.aspx?GroupId=91&MID=668

Moynihan, D. P. (2007). The reality of results: Managing for results in state and local government. In P. Ingraham (Ed.), *In pursuit of performance: Management systems in state and local government* (pp. 151–177). Baltimore, MD: The Johns Hopkins University Press.

NASPAA Commission on Peer Review & Accreditation. (2009). NASPAA Standards 2009: Accreditation Standards for Master's Programs. National Association of Schools of Public Affairs and Administration. Retrieved from http://www.naspaa.org/accreditation/doc/NS2009FinalVote10.16.2009.pdf

Newcomer, K. (2001). Tracking and probing program performance: Fruitful path or blind alley for evaluation professionals? *American Journal of Evaluation, 22,* 337–341.

Patrizi, P. A. (2010). Strategy evaluation: Emerging processes and methods. In P. A. Patrizi & M. Q. Patton (Eds.), *Evaluating strategy. New Directions for Evaluation, 128,* 87–102.

Patton, M. Q. (2008). *Utilization-focused evaluation* (4th ed.). Los Angeles, CA: Sage.

Poister, T. H. (2004). Performance monitoring. In J. S. Wholey, H. Hatry, & K. E. Newcomer (Eds.), *Handbook of practical program evaluation* (2nd ed., pp. 98–125). San Francisco, CA: John Wiley & Sons.

Strengthening evaluation effectiveness. (2011, January). Symposium conducted at The Trachtenberg School of Public Policy and Public Administration sponsored by The Evaluator's Institute, the Midge Smith Center for Evaluation Effectiveness, the Washington Evaluators, and TSPPPA. Remarks by Harry Hatry, Gary Henry, Kathryn Newcomer, and Ted Poister.

Wholey, J. S. (1986). Using evaluation to improve government performance. *American Journal of Evaluation, 7,* 5–13.

Wholey, J. S. (1996). Formative and summative evaluation: Related issues in performance measurement. *American Journal of Evaluation, 17,* 145–149.

Wholey, J. (2001). Managing for results: Roles for evaluators in a new management era. *American Journal of Evaluation, 22*(3), 343–347.

TERESA M. DERRICK-MILLS is a doctoral candidate specializing in program evaluation in the Trachtenberg School at The George Washington University.

Hoffman, K. A. (2011). Evaluation of multinational programs: Value and challenges. In
S. Mathison (Ed.), *Really new directions in evaluation: Young evaluators' perspectives. New
Directions for Evaluation, 131,* 91–96.

14

Evaluation of Multinational Programs: Value and Challenges

Kim A. Hoffman

Abstract

*Opportunities for the evaluation of multinational projects offer potential for
insights into project operations and effects across sites, cultures, nations, and
regions. The author discusses the value of building robust multinational evaluations, practical considerations for gaining ethical clearances in diverse settings,
and ways to accommodate projects with varied implementation processes and
goals.* © Wiley Periodicals, Inc., and the American Evaluation Association.

Unique challenges are associated with evaluating multisite projects
(Straw & Herrell, 2002). Cross-site assessment and comparative
analyses challenges are even more dynamic when multisite evaluation includes multiple nations, each with unique histories, institutions, cultures, and governments. Growing international momentum for multination
initiatives portends the need for robust evaluation tools and approaches
applicable across varied sociopolitical settings. The potential for insights
into project operations and effects is balanced with complexities associated
with cost and scope.

Value of Building Robust Multinational Evaluations

Multinational evaluations usually have defined agendas and common measurement of agreed indicators, although specific indicators may vary by

country. A global/lead evaluator monitors the achievement of specific targets for each individual country and provides coordination to project partners. Such projects often include a monitoring element in addition to the evaluation of project outcomes, referred to as monitoring and evaluation (M&E). The monitoring component tracks the degree of implementation compliance and provides timely information for any needed protocol adjustments. Reporting on effects without determining if the intervention was implemented as it was designed can lead to faulty conclusions (Rehle, Saidel, Mills, & Magnani, 2001). Monitoring data do not adequately address "whether, how, and why a program works" (Peersman & Rugg, 2004, p. 141) and therefore are coupled with an evaluation protocol. M&E provides accountability for program and policy decisions and sometimes performance-based funding disbursements. The concepts provided in this article are equally applicable for M&E projects, though the more general term of *evaluation* is used.

Notions of evaluation and project monitoring have general acceptance at the global level, but country-level understandings may vary. A global/lead evaluator may need to provide conceptual training and technical assistance to project partners and data collectors. Although these roles may not be explicit in the terms of employment, without such efforts the evaluation may not yield optimal results. Many countries have almost no access to vitally needed M&E technical assistance (Wilson, 2004). In an assessment of more than 100 governments implementing HIV/AIDS prevention and treatment programs, 75% of respondent countries report "inadequate M & E capacity was one of their most difficult challenges" (Massoud, De Lay, & Carael, 2004, p. 60).

Global/lead evaluators can build capacity with local collaborators through an initial training by using—or explaining how to use—Voice over Internet Protocol (VoIP) service. Skype is a low/no-cost method of sending files, instant messaging, and conducting conference and video calls. Evaluation staff may be required to communicate across vast distances; VoIP provides a nice way to build relationships between individuals who may never meet in person. Some collaborators with limited English skills may feel more comfortable using instant messaging rather than voice communication, which affords time for reading, understanding, and responding. If the quality of the voice transmission is poor, instant messaging is a good second choice and is superior to e-mail in many cases where iterative and/or time-sensitive problem solving is required. Although it is obvious, understanding time-zone differences is vital for setting VoIP meeting times, especially in countries that are a quarter or half hour off GMT, have both horizontal and vertical time zones, or are subject to Daylight Saving/summer time changes. An excellent resource for this type of information can be found at www.worldtimezone.com/faq.html.

NEW DIRECTIONS FOR EVALUATION • DOI: 10.1002/ev

Ethical Clearances

Gaining ethical or Institutional Review Board (IRB) clearances for multinational evaluations can be complex. Depending on the type and location of the research, the Common Rule, Federal Wide Assurance Considerations, and/or the Declaration of Helsinki will apply. In the case that a global/lead evaluator is not allowed to open country-level applications, local investigators with the proper credentials will need to be appointed. Building adequate time into the evaluation time line is vital, especially for initial review, which can take months. Researching the appropriate regulatory committee before submitting a request can avoid using a month or more in the queue with one committee only to be told that it is necessary to use a different one.

It is generally advised to gain sponsor and/or lead investigator country approvals, even if all research will be carried on outside of it. Many protocols fall into the minimal risk category and are eligible for expedited review. Something to consider is whether the condition of minimal risk is true in the local context, particularly for vulnerable populations. Gaining sponsor country IRB approvals before seeking country-level approvals may be required and may speed the process of approval in host countries. In certain cases it may be necessary to transfer IRB authority to local sites and a memorandum of understanding that lists the obligations of participating institutions should be sought. In these cases it may be possible for the global/lead evaluator to (a) call or Skype into local review committee meetings, (b) be copied on correspondence, and (c) ask to see copies of approval notices. Although a relatively recent development, a U.S.-based IRB can develop dialogue with a participating country IRB to sort through complexities and come to agreements.

In some countries, a national regulatory system may not be evident. An excellent source of information is the 2011 International Compilation of Human Research Protections, available on the Office for Human Research Protections website (http://www.hhs.gov/ohrp/international/index.html). This document provides an overview and links to human subjects' entities and guidelines in 101 countries. In some low-resource countries, regulatory bodies may not officially exist. In these cases it is appropriate to seek documentation with the governing bodies (credible, official agencies) that can sign off on the evaluation protocol.

Finally, informed-consent documents for respondents should be simple and clear. Good translation is important for any informed-consent documentation (as well as all of the instruments) and forward and backward translation is advised. Respondents should be able to understand what the project is about and why it is being undertaken. Language should be clear about respondents' rights to discontinue participation at any time without repercussions. This component must also be understood by data collectors administering the informed consent/questionnaires, as they may feel (a) pressure to meet M&E participation numbers or (b) that the participation of a reluctant respondent is "in their best interest."

Addressing Project Variation

Although the primary objective of a program may be common across countries, features of the initiative may be country dependent. For example, a project may have an overarching goal of improving the delivery of drug treatment; in Haiti, those funds may be used for rebuilding earthquake-damaged physical infrastructure, while in Brazil the funds may be used to train practitioners in evidence-based treatment practices. What constitutes a site can also vary. Given the previous example, some sites may be well-established drug-treatment centers whereas others may be primary health-care sites with no previous experience delivering drug treatment. Existing centers may be asked to implement a new methadone maintenance program, whereas the primary health-care sites will train existing personnel in simple drug screening and brief intervention techniques. Geographical complexities can also occur: One country may have one or two large project sites in easily accessible urban centers; another may have multiple, smaller sites scattered across rural, hard-to-access areas. These considerations should be taken into account for (a) project budget and time line and (b) terms of employment with local collaborators so that responsibilities are clearly defined and remuneration is fair, given variation in workload between countries.

Building Collaborations

Local stakeholders and experts can provide input to the evaluation team during the development of the evaluation design. These epistemic communities can inform the global/lead evaluator about circumstances within their countries that require protocol adaptations. Involving collaborators in decisions provides insights, ideas, and buy-in from critical groups. Seeking input during planning and execution grants an opportunity to assess any resistance, diagnose problems with the protocol, and assuage fears about cross-site comparisons (Fredericks, Carman, & Birkland, 2002).

Efficient and cost-effective data collection can occur by employing a network of country-level data collectors. In this model, the lead evaluator hires data collectors in each country to implement the protocol within their respective countries and report data to the global/lead evaluator. The use of country-level data collectors can lessen the traditional tension observed between the "intrusive foreign evaluator" and the host-country participants. The issue of whether the collectors are considered "insiders" or "outsiders" in all of the regions they will be responsible for should be considered to reduce potential resistance from project staff or respondents. Country data collectors should provide memos or logs to the global/lead evaluator documenting deviations from the protocol, a description of why/when things went awry, if/how problems were ameliorated, and any anecdotal information that might be of value. These qualitative sources of information can be a resource to the lead evaluator when results are unexpected.

NEW DIRECTIONS FOR EVALUATION • DOI: 10.1002/ev

An extension of this model includes a train-the-trainers approach: The global/lead evaluator delivers substantive training and materials to national evaluators, who then instruct within-country, site-level data collectors. The national evaluator manages the site-level data collectors and is ultimately responsible for their timely and accurate reporting of data. National data collectors should be able to speak the language of the global/lead evaluator and also any languages/dialects within the country where the project is being implemented.

Decreasing Unnecessary Noise in the Data Set

Multination evaluation data sets are susceptible to noise introduced from country-level variables beyond the evaluator's control: national or territorial conflicts, natural disasters, funds that are not reaching participating sites, the misunderstandings of implementers, etc. Some of these issues can only be addressed via disclosure at the reporting stage, but some problems can be minimized. When possible, national data collectors should be screened for prior training in evaluation methods and the global/lead evaluator should frequently perform checks for compliance during the study period. The methodological soundness of an evaluation can be severely impacted by even basic problems, such as failing to adequately report pre-/postintervention measures (Peersman & Rugg, 2004). Variance associated with misunderstandings about the timing of data collection can be avoided by requiring collaborators to use tracking tools. For example, a lead evaluator can create country- and/or site-specific Excel worksheets with time lines and checklists for each data collector. The evaluation time line must take into consideration the impact that local customs/observances/holidays will have on activities.

Conclusion

Multinational evaluation takes into account local variations while providing an opportunity for global comparisons. Because of the cost and time typically associated with these projects, challenges abound. Evaluators should assess a variety of issues during the design and implementation of an evaluation protocol, including ethical clearances, variation in program implementation, input from stakeholders, and steps that can be taken to minimize noise in the data set. Partnerships, communication, and coordination are successful mechanisms to achieve rigorous multination evaluation goals.

References

Fredericks, K., Carman, J., & Birkland, T. (2002). Program evaluation in a challenging authorizing environment: Intergovernmental and interorganizational factors. *New Directions for Evaluation, 95*, 5–21.

NEW DIRECTIONS FOR EVALUATION • DOI: 10.1002/ev

Ginsburg, A., & Rhett, N. (2003). Building a better body of evidence: New opportunities to strengthen evaluation utilization. *American Journal of Evaluation, 24*(4), 489–498.

Massoud, N., De Lay, P., & Carael, M. (2004). Has the United Nations General Assembly Special Session on HIV/AIDS made a difference? *New Directions for Evaluation, 103,* 49–64.

Peersman, G., & Rugg, D. (2004). Intervention research and program evaluation: The need to move beyond monitoring. *New Directions for Evaluation, 103,* 141–158.

Rehle, T., Saidel, T., Mills, S., & Magnani, R. (2001). Conceptual approach and framework for monitoring and evaluation. In T. Rehle, T. Saidel, S. Mills, & R. Magnani (Eds.), *Evaluating programs for HIV/AIDS prevention and care in developing countries: A handbook for program managers and decision makers.* Arlington, VA: Family Health International.

Straw, R., & Herrell, J. (2002). A framework for understanding and improving multisite evaluations. *New Directions for Evaluation, 94,* 5–16.

Wilson, D. (2004). World Bank contribution to building national HIV/AIDS monitoring and evaluation capacity in Africa. *New Directions for Evaluation, 103,* 101–115.

KIM A. HOFFMAN is a senior research associate at Oregon Health and Science University and the independent evaluator for Treatnet II, a United Nations Office on Drugs and Crime intervention to improve delivery of drug treatment in 20 countries.

Jansen van Rensburg, M. S. (2011). Using organizational memory directories to analyze networks. In S. Mathison (Ed.), *Really new directions in evaluation: Young evaluators' perspectives*. New Directions for Evaluation, 131, 97–102.

15

Using Organizational Memory Directories to Analyze Networks

Madri S. Jansen van Rensburg

Abstract

This chapter describes the value of organizational memory (OM) directories and networks to improve evaluations and monitoring activities with the use of a case study. Networking within and between organizations is considered increasingly important, and organizational memory and the directory of the memory are needed to access these networks and determine their influence. Networks— social and business—and the ability to document and map networks and their influence are progressively becoming generally more important, including in evaluation studies. Future focus on networks and OM will make it possible to identify key and more-distant stakeholders and beneficiaries, and to examine the networks to enable reliability of impact evaluations. © Wiley Periodicals, Inc., and the American Evaluation Association.

O rganizational memory (OM) does not only lie in the information stored by individual memories, but also in the "directories" held by the individuals that can identify the existence, location, and means of retrieval of memory (Wegner, Erber, & Raymond, 1991). Research on OM is important not only for critical incidents and disasters, but also to enable learning in organizations that will lead to more efficient decision making. Learning organizations are organizations that base decisions on past experience (Huber, 1991; Senge, 2006). Evaluations enable nongovernmental organizations (NGOs) to learn from their experiences and OM, and access

New Directions for Evaluation, no. 131, Fall 2011 © Wiley Periodicals, Inc., and the American Evaluation Association. Published online in Wiley Online Library (wileyonlinelibrary.com) • DOI: 10.1002/ev.385

to the memory through directories is crucial. Access to the memory and investigation of the directories are needed to enhance evaluation activities, especially regarding contextual factors.

Organizational Memory

Organizational memory can be defined as "the means by which knowledge from the past is brought to bear on present activities, thus resulting in higher or lower levels of organizational effectiveness" (Stein, 1995, p. 22), and consists of both explicit (as expressed in policies and documents) and tacit (insight and skills embedded in individuals) memory (Connell, Klein, & Powell, 2003). Stein (1995) distinguishes four types of OM, combining explicit and tacit memory and individual and social memory, as described by Corbett (2000). The four types are *conscious* (explicit individual), *automatic* (implicit individual), *objectified* (explicit social), and *collective* (implicit social) memory. Walsh and Ungson (1991, pp. 63–67) described OM as consisting of "five storage bins": individuals, organizational culture, processes of transformation, organizational structures (roles), and workplace ecology. Olivera (2000) added information technologies to these storage bins.

In addition to structure, process is also important when studying OM. The different processes of OM include the acquisition, retention, retrieval, and maintenance (prevention of loss and decay of OM) of information (Stein, 1995; Walsh & Ungson, 1991). Organizational learning occurs when knowledge is spread through the organization through memory (Jackson, 2007).

Metamemory and Directories

It is important to consider the metamemory (or directories) of the OM (Hamidi & Jusoff, 2009; Nevo & Wand, 2005). OM of individual group members has two components: (a) information stored in individual memories, and (b) the directories held by individuals that identify the existence, location, and means of retrieval of information held by the other individuals (Anand, Manz, & Glick, 1998). Similarly, Schwartz (1998) describes organizational memories as a combination of two main components: (a) a knowledge base, which contains the content or knowledge that is of value to the organization, and (b) a well-defined set of metaknowledge, which is used to determine how and when the knowledge or content should be applied.

An important distinction is also made between internal memory (memory held by group members personally) and external memory (memory not within personal memory of the group, but that can be retrieved when necessary) (Wegner, 1986). According to Anand et al. (1998, p. 797) "directories are idiosyncratic information items that inform group members about the existence and location of external information, as well as the means of retrieving such information." Information in directories includes labels. These labels are held idiosyncratically and play a critical role in the retrieval of information. Information can be accessed easily if group members all use the same labels to tag information in the memory. External OM can only be accessed through communication (Anand et al., 1998). Directories include electronic indices (including management information systems) and individuals, such as administrative staff, who, because of long-term service, often have extended networks and knowledge of information sources. This not only has implications for investment in sophisticated technology, but also needs soft skills in building and maintaining important relationships with key gatekeepers and those holding the metamemory and directories.

Group members must first locate memory before they can use it. Locating information may take two paths: (a) members might have directories that identify the correct person with the information, or (b) the member does not have a relevant directory and must first search for the directory. In the first instance communicating the information will be the next step, while in the second instance a search process needs to be conducted first. In this regard, the current developments in computers, intranets (used to access organizational directories or to broadcast a request for information), and search engines are very useful (Anand et al., 1998).

The directories of NGOs (as providing access to the organizational memory) are closely linked to the social and business networks of the organizations, especially in large (regional or international) intermediary and donor organizations. Utilizing the directories allows investigation of interorganizational networks and relationships that are important to understand contextual issues in evaluations.

An Illustration of the Value of Understanding Organizational Memory

A single explanatory historical case study of OM was conducted in a regional intermediary organization that has completed all the developmental phases, including startup, expansion, consolidation, and closeout (Al-Talal, 2004; Edwards & Fowler, 2002).

The case was a regional NGO working in HIV prevention and mitigation. Project Support Group Southern Africa (PSG) started in 1985 in association with the Department of Psychology of the University of Zimbabwe. It grew from a local (Zimbabwean) NGO to one working in nine Southern African Development Community (SADC) countries. PSG provided funding and technical support to 36 partner NGOs and community-based organizations (CBOs), but closed down during 2008 because of a loss of donor funding. Using PSG to study OM provides an opportunity to study the impact of memory development and possible memory loss. Information was gathered by making use of a multisource approach, including data sources such as documentation, archival records, 47 interviews (with current and past staff members, beneficiaries, donors, and other stakeholders), direct observations (e.g., the hard copies and electronic copies of the explicit memory), participant observations (during board, management, and staff meetings), and physical artifacts.

Using Directories to Access Organizational Memory

Organizational memory and the directories to access the memory should receive more attention in general management of NGOs and evaluations of activities, outcomes, and impact (Girard, 2009; Hamidi & Jusoff, 2009; Nevo & Wand, 2005; Wegner, 1986). Access to the memory is virtually impossible without the directories (Anand et al., 1998). They enable access to the networks (and individual and interorganizational relationships) and the OM stored in individuals (and hard copies). Investigation of the different developmental phases of PSG showed clearly that there was a definite shift of the perceived importance of different individual organizational memories and directories to access the OM. During the startup phase the founder was the most critical person, whereas during the phase of expansion of target areas, within Zimbabwe and Southern Africa, all individuals (a small core group of three individuals) held the OM. When functions expanded and the staff complement increased, the OM was found in the managers of the different units. During consolidation the memory was located in all staff members, and access to the OM was through directories (individuals who were not necessarily managers, but experts and also administrative and IT staff). During the later phases of the consolidation and the closeout phase, the focus shifted to metamemory and directories.

The directories of PSG were in the form of previous staff members, beneficiary organizations, and hard and electronic indices of documents and key role players. Understanding the directories and the changes in the directories during the different phases of development of PSG increased the access to the OM and increased the evaluation of the influence of PSG during its existence. The directories allowed access to networks that were not directly evident from the immediate relationships. For example, the list of previous staff members provided access to individuals who knew previous suppliers of the organization who provided insight into the reputation of the organization at a specific time of development. This is one type of interorganizational relationship. Another is the relationship between PSG and its beneficiary organizations and between the beneficiary organizations.

Interorganizational networks are very important for regional intermediary organizations such as PSG, as their main function is to increase the combined impact of the grassroots organizations that are best suited for community responses. Evaluating relationships and networks is difficult without access to the networks. The networks in turn are part of the OM, which is accessed through the directories. Normally the involvement of networks can be seen either as an input from the acting organization or as a strategy to implement the innovation (Raynor, 2010). In the case of PSG, it appeared to be both an input and a strategy.

What this case study illustrates is the importance of directories to access the OM and therefore the networks and relationships of the organization being evaluated. Understanding the OM and networks facilitates the evaluation and also provides a better understanding of the contextual issues (especially changes over time as reflected by the relationships). Social network analysis can be greatly enhanced by understanding directories and OM.

Conclusion

It is evident that the directory of the OM is a critical factor when accessing the context of NGO activities. In order to perform valid contextual evaluations increased awareness of the directories and associated networks are crucial, especially when considering temporal changes as the directories change during different organizational developmental phases. The memory of PSG was not lost and was recoverable through the different directories. The memory was not genetically transferred to the surviving "offspring," but will remain in artifacts, documents, and individuals as long as the directories remain available.

References

Al-Talal, B. B. (2004). *Rethinking an NGO: Development, donors and civil society in Jordan.* London, United Kingdom: IB Taris.

Anand, V., Manz, C. C., & Glick, W. H. (1998). An organizational memory approach to information management. *Academy of Management Review, 23*(4), 796–809.

Connell, N. A. D., Klein, J. H., & Powell, P. L. (2003). It's tacit knowledge but not as we know it: Redirecting the search for knowledge. *Journal of Operational Research Society, 54,* 140–152.

Corbett, J. M. (2000). On being an elephant in the age of oblivion. Computer-based information systems and organisational memory. *Information Technology & People, 13*(4), 282.

Edwards, M., & Fowler, A. (2002). *The Earthscan Reader on NGO management.* London, United Kingdom: Earthscan Publications.

Girard, J. P. (2009). *Building organizational memories: Will you know what you knew?* Hershey, PA: IGI-Global.

Hamidi, S. R., & Jusoff, K. (2009). The characteristic and success factors of an organizational memory information system. *Computer and Information Science, 2*(1), 142–151.

Huber, G. P. (1991). Organizational learning: The contributing processes and the literatures. *Organization, 2*(1), 88–115.

Jackson, T. W. (2007). Applying autopoiesis to knowledge management in organisations. *Journal of Knowledge Management, 11*(3), 78–91.

Nevo, D., & Wand, Y. (2005). Organizational memory information systems: A transactive memory approach. *Decision Support Systems, 39*(4), 549–562.

Olivera, F. (2000). Memory systems in organisations: An empirical investigation of mechanisms of knowledge collection, storage and access. *Journal of Management Studies, 37*(6), 811–832.

Raynor, J. (2010, 7 December). *Evaluating networks and partnerships.* MyMandE Webinar. Retrieved from http://www.mymande.org/?q=evaluating_networks_and_part nerships

Schwartz, D. G. (1998). Shared semantics and the use of organizational memories for e-mail communications. *Journal of Internet Research, 8*(5), 434–441.

Senge, P. M. (2006). *The fifth discipline: The art & practice of the learning organization.* New York, NY: Doubleday.

Stein, E. W. (1995). Organizational memory: Review of concepts and recommendations for management. *International Journal of Information Management, 15*(1), 17–32.

Walsh, J. P., & Ungson, G. R. (1991). Organizational memory. *Academy of Management Review, 16*(1), 57–91.

Wegner, D. M. (1986). Transactive memory: A contemporary analysis of the group mind. In B. Mullen & G. R. Goethals (Eds.), *Theories of group behaviour.* New York, NY: Springer.

Wegner, D. M., Erber, R., & Raymond, P. (1991). Transactive memory in close relationships. *Journal of Personality and Social Behaviour, 61,* 923–929.

MADRI S. JANSEN VAN RENSBURG is a research psychologist conducting research and evaluation studies with NGOs in the Southern African region.

Price, K. M. (2011). The evolution of understanding: Positioning evaluation within a comprehensive performance management system. In S. Mathison (Ed.), *Really new directions in evaluation: Young evaluators' perspectives. New Directions for Evaluation, 131,* 103–109.

16

The Evolution of Understanding: Positioning Evaluation Within a Comprehensive Performance Management System

Kelci M. Price

Abstract

Although performance management has become a common organizational practice, in many cases it has not resulted in substantial program improvement or organizational learning. The author discusses two issues related to performance management systems that are of key concern to evaluators: (a) evaluation is often excluded from these systems in favor of monitoring data, and (b) performance management systems tend to focus on the creation of data rather than its use. The author discusses the complementary roles of evaluation and monitoring data, and highlights some ways in which evaluation can help improve performance management systems. © Wiley Periodicals, Inc., and the American Evaluation Association.

Performance management, results-based management, evidence-based policy making, and data-driven decision making are terms that have become ubiquitous, emerging in areas as diverse as education, transportation, and international aid. At their core, these concepts refer to the idea that by systematically gathering and using data we can make better decisions, which will ultimately result in improved programs and better outcomes.

Program evaluation has a key role to play in performance management (PM). Though considerations around the development of a quality PM system are numerous, I focus on two major issues of concern to evaluators. First, with the growing focus on high-stakes accountability and demands for rapid conclusions about program effectiveness, PM systems are often based only on monitoring data (simple quantitative indicators of program performance), whereas evaluation is excluded because it is viewed as too complex and untimely. Second, most PM systems are focused on creating data rather than using data, even though it has become clear that producing copious amounts of data is not sufficient to generate programmatic improvement.

Evaluators are well positioned to address both these issues. I compare and contrast monitoring and evaluation data and discuss the different questions that each addresses as part of a comprehensive PM system. The discussion then highlights some ways in which evaluators can help improve systems of performance management.

Promise and Practice of Performance Management

At its core, the concept of PM is one of *systematic learning*. In practice, this generally means that program activities, outputs, and outcomes are measured and the information is used to guide decisions. Such decisions may include ways that the program should be modified, resources reallocated, or organizational strategy changed. Though the practice of PM has existed in different forms for at least 30 years (Perrin, 1998), there has recently been a renewed focus on PM among government agencies, nonprofits, and foundations. Demands for PM are generally associated with calls for more informed decision making, increased transparency, and accountability for outcomes (e.g., USAID, 2011).

Despite its popularity, PM has largely failed to produce a sea change of practice (Perrin, 1998). One reason for this is that the current paradigm of PM frequently excludes rigorous program evaluation (Blalock, 1999). As pressures for accountability and transparency have increased, organizations have often turned to simple dashboards and scorecards to track, communicate, and assess program outcomes. Such a system seems to offer simple answers to complex questions of program implementation and effectiveness. Indeed, Newcomer and Scheirer (2001) found that many program managers used data from performance monitoring as the sole way of evaluating their program. This represents an impoverished concept of program evaluation, because monitoring data cannot address crucial questions about why certain outcomes occurred or whether the program caused those outcomes. Without exploring these questions, decision makers lack the information they need to know what changes should be implemented, and whether a program is producing expected outcomes.

Another issue with many PM systems is that they focus on the creation of data, grounded in the belief that increasing the availability of data will heighten accountability, and lead to improved performance and outcomes. However, research has indicated that simply increasing the amount of available data is

NEW DIRECTIONS FOR EVALUATION • DOI: 10.1002/ev

Table 16.1. Comparison of Evaluation and Monitoring Data

	Evaluation	Monitoring
Frequency of data collection	Lower	Higher
Tailoring of information	Specific to the evaluation questions	Usually standardized across time and sites
Sample/scope	Sample of units	Population (all units)
Methods	Mixed methods, quantitative, qualitative	Quantitative
Analyses	Descriptive, inferential, synthesis of sources	Descriptive
Outcomes assessed	Results, net impact	Results
Attribution of outcomes	Test causal hypotheses, account for selection bias	Causality assumed
Communication strategies	Reports, briefs, presentations, facilitated discussions, and so on	Simple documents, dashboards
Availability of information	Less frequent	Potentially real-time

not sufficient for improvement. A report from the Government Accountability Office (GAO, 1995) noted, ". . . lack of information does not appear to be the main problem. Rather, the problem seems to be that available information is not organized and communicated effectively" (p. 39). In the absence of processes and structures to support the use of data in decision making, the actual production of data is unlikely to improve practice.

Complementary Knowledge: Monitoring and Evaluation

Monitoring and evaluation data serve as "complementary forms of knowledge production" (Nielsen & Ejler, 2008, p. 171) within a comprehensive PM system, but there are some important differences between these types of data. Although there are not always hard lines between monitoring and evaluation, some major distinctions are presented in Table 16.1. Performance monitoring tends to make up the core data that are regularly collected to inform program operations. In contrast, evaluation studies tend to provide a deeper level of knowledge about what is happening, why it is happening, and whether outcomes can be attributed to the program.

Because of their characteristics, monitoring and evaluation are suited to answering different types of questions, some of which are highlighted in Table 16.2. Monitoring data is particularly appropriate for addressing operational questions around program functioning, implementation, and movement toward expected results. It plays a crucial role in program management by identifying site-specific issues, findings successes and challenges in implementation, and highlighting general trends or results across time.

Table 16.2. Possible Questions Addressed by Evaluation and Monitoring Data

	Evaluation	Monitoring
Program theory	What are the program's strategic goals? What is the program theory?	N/A
Strategic and program planning	Are the program's strategies and intended objectives still relevant? What strategies may be most effective in the future?	N/A
Program delivery and implementation	What are some areas needing improvement? How can the program be changed in order to improve it? How do contextual factors affect implementation?	What does progress toward goals look like weekly/monthly/and so on? What issues of implementation need to be further assessed?
Assessment of results	Why did these outcomes occur? What unanticipated results occurred?	What are the outcomes of participants? Which programs have outcomes worth further exploration?
Attribution of impact	Are the outcomes the result of the program?	N/A

In contrast, evaluation tends to focus not only on what is happening, but also why. The question of "why" is a critical one and cannot be addressed through the simple quantitative indicators used for monitoring data. Evaluation studies tend to use mixed methods to gain a deeper understanding of the program, often considering how context has impacted a program's functioning. This knowledge is crucial for providing decision makers with relevant information about what specific changes are needed for program improvement. Equally important is evaluation's ability to assess impact and causality, which cannot be addressed by monitoring data. Evaluation studies tend to be most useful for understanding the overall functioning of the program, providing information on what specific changes could lead to program improvement, and making decisions at the programmatic level.

Evaluation: Improving Learning and Data Use in Performance Management

There is no simple recipe or template to create a comprehensive system of PM, though good discussions of PM's core components can be found in Nielsen and Ejler (2008), Blalock (1999), and Mayne (2007). This section highlights a few key ways that evaluators can help create better PM systems.

Implement Learning Mechanisms

Opportunity. One of the major problems with many PM systems is the lack of mechanisms to incorporate data into decision-making processes (GAO, 1995). Evaluators should work with clients to institutionalize feedback loops so data are regularly discussed in a thoughtful way by both managers and program staff (Nielsen & Ejler, 2008). Learning occurs best when stakeholders have a chance to analyze data, synthesize results, and critically assess findings. Evaluators are uniquely skilled in guiding stakeholders through discussions of available data with reference to their key questions. It is important to avoid the ritualistic use of data that does not promote learning; a good litmus test of learning is whether stakeholders are able to explain what they learned from the data, and how their actions were informed (or not) by the findings.

Capacity. Part of engaging staff in learning includes capacity building. Although the amount of data available about programs has increased exponentially, managers and program staff may not have the skills necessary to interpret data and apply it to their decision process. Evaluators can play a key role in capacity building through both formal and informal interaction, including modeling evaluative thinking skills (e.g., asking meaningful questions), helping stakeholders consider alternative explanations for findings, and brainstorming with clients the ways in which the findings could inform practice.

Innovate Evaluation Practice

Evaluators should also focus on how evaluation can be a better contributor of information as part of a PM system. Two core considerations are suggested here.

Responsiveness. Evaluation often seems unresponsive to emergent questions and issues (Bamberger, 2008; Nielsen & Ejler, 2008). Although evaluators continue to grapple with how to incorporate rapid data collection and analysis into existing evaluation plans in a meaningful and rigorous way, evaluators should be open to finding ways to meet emergent needs. Even a quick survey, a small number of interviews, or analysis of a subset of existing data can make an important contribution when stakeholders have an imminent decision to make.

Meaningful reporting. Evaluation reports should be structured to provide clear answers to evaluation questions, rather than separating findings by data type or instrument (Davidson, 2007). In many instances, addressing evaluation questions will involve synthesizing findings from different components of the PM system, such as evaluation and monitoring data. Reporting should also include summaries and recommendations that relate to what can be learned from the data and how the data can be used to inform decision making, as opposed to focusing on limitations of the evaluation study.

Accept Ambiguity

PM is not simply about collecting more data, crafting measures, or creating systems. Rather, it is about cultivating habits of mind. The goal of PM should be to instill an "attitude of wisdom—the ability to act with knowledge while doubting what you know" (Pfeffer & Sutton, 2006, p. 174). Stakeholders are often keenly disappointed when they find that even after reviewing all available data, questions remain and the path forward is not clear. As Mayne (2007) points out, data from PM have "been cast by some as a panacea for improving management and budgeting: users of performance information will have at their fingertips everything they need to know to manage, budget or hold to account. Such is not and will not be the case" (p. 93). Evaluators can play a crucial role in helping stakeholders understand the promise and limitations of PM, and can help organizations learn to be more comfortable making decisions in the context of inadequate and incomplete information.

Moving Forward

PM systems can be of considerable value to organizations when they provide appropriate information to answer stakeholder questions, and when they incorporate structures to encourage thoughtful and reflective use of data. Evaluators are uniquely qualified to help organizations identify what data are needed to answer their questions, and to build organizational capacity to assess data critically and integrate it into decision processes. By focusing on best practices in how evaluation data are produced, disseminated, and utilized, evaluators can be key drivers of more useful PM systems in the future.

References

Bamberger, M. (2008). Enhancing the utilization of evaluations for evidence-based policy making. In *Bridging the gap: The role of monitoring and evaluation in evidence-based policy making* (pp. 120–142). Geneva, Switzerland: UNICEF.

Blalock, A. B. (1999). Evaluation research and the performance management movement: From estrangement to useful integration? *Evaluation, 5*(2), 117–149.

Davidson, J. E. (2007). Unlearning some of our social scientist habits. *Journal of Multi-Disciplinary Evaluation, 4*(8), iii–vi.

Government Accountability Office. (1995). *Program evaluation: Improving the flow of information to the Congress* (No. GAO/PEMD-95-1). Washington, DC: GAO. Retrieved from http://www.gao.gov/products/PEMD-95-1

Mayne, J. (2007). Challenges and lessons in implementing results-based management. *Evaluation, 13*(1), 87–109.

Newcomer, K. E., & Scheirer, M. A. (2001). *Using evaluation to support performance management: A guide for federal executives.* Innovations: Management Series. Arlington, VA: The PricewaterhouseCoopers Endowment for the Business of Government.

Nielsen, S. B., & Ejler, N. (2008). Improving performance?: Exploring the complementarities between evaluation and performance management. *Evaluation, 14*(2), 171–192.

Perrin, B. (1998). Effective use and misuse of performance measurement. *American Journal of Evaluation, 19*(3), 367–379.

Pfeffer, J., & Sutton, R. I. (2006). *Hard facts, dangerous half-truths and total nonsense: Profiting from evidence-based management* (1st ed.). Boston, MA: Harvard Business Press.

USAID. (2011). *Learning from experience: USAID evaluation policy.* Washington, DC: Bureau for Policy, Planning, and Learning. Retrieved from http://www.usaid.gov /evaluation/USAID_Evaluation_Policy.pdf

KELCI M. PRICE is a senior evaluator with The Evaluation Center, a nonprofit evaluation consulting group in the School of Education and Human Development at the University of Colorado, Denver.

NEW DIRECTIONS FOR EVALUATION • DOI: 10.1002/ev

Wilson, K. A. (2011). Effectiveness engineering: Vistas of opportunity beyond merit, worth, and significance. In S. Mathison (Ed.), *Really new directions in evaluation: Young evaluators' perspectives. New Directions for Evaluation, 131,* 111–116.

17

Effectiveness Engineering: Vistas of Opportunity Beyond Merit, Worth, and Significance

Kurt A. Wilson

Abstract

Practicing evaluators can be understood as representing the "brand" of evaluation, and as such face challenges with the negative connotations and overall confusion surrounding the field. Effectiveness engineering is presented as a sensitizing concept, a new way of seeing the subset of evaluation approaches that engage goals expanding beyond a determination of merit, worth, or significance. Emerging methodologies addressing systems and complexity, and two portals from Google that provide free data, are suggested as especially relevant resources for those that resonate with the "effectiveness engineering" concept. © Wiley Periodicals, Inc., and the American Evaluation Association.

Evaluation has a branding problem. The "brand" of evaluation, that bit of mental and emotional real estate related to the word and overall concept, unfortunately suffers the worst problems a brand can have: both negative emotional associations and ambiguity or lack of clarity. For many people the term carries emotional toxins, reminders of threatening school exams or employee reviews, for example. The ambiguity, or lack of general-public clarity about evaluation, flows from the uniquely broad territory that the brand of evaluation covers: Evaluation is simultaneously an aspect of basic human cognition (anyone can *evaluate* his or her options) as well as a specific profession (only a few people are *evaluators*). Furthermore, variants of the term can be a verb (*to evaluate*), noun (an *evaluation*), adverb (think *evaluatively*), and adjective (*evaluative* terms). Thus, although evaluation is a transdiscipline like logic or statistics (Mathison, 2005), it is also substantially broader, and consequently more elusive, than its transdisciplinary peers.

The baggage and confusion surrounding the term have frankly come as a surprise. I am currently a second-year student in the Interdisciplinary PhD in Evaluation program at Western Michigan University, and for the last 12 years have worked in nonprofit branding, film production, and Web development. I entered the field of evaluation with implicit expectations that clients and friends would match my excitement about the world of evaluation. How wrong I was. Because of both the emotional toxins and the confusion noted above, I now reference *evaluation* as specifically as possible, typically noting "the determination of merit, worth or significance" (Scriven, 2011) as the central concern. At the same time, I have developed a deeper appreciation for the much broader value evaluators can provide; the many interconnected services, goals, and evaluation approaches that ripple out from that central point. For example, developmental evaluation (Patton, 2011), empowerment evaluation (Fetterman, 2000), or critical theory evaluation (Mathison, 2005) utilize the perspective, training, and experience of evaluators toward broader (and sometimes altogether different) goals than determining merit, worth, or significance.

These "broad goal" evaluation approaches are the focus of this article. I recognize that there are longstanding debates about boundaries and definitions within the field, so I hope to tread lightly and not denigrate any approach or perspective. Instead, my goal is to provide a new term and way of thinking about the breadth of evaluation approaches as a sensitizing concept, with the intent of offering a "way of seeing, organizing, and understanding experience . . ." that may "deepen perception . . . or provide starting points for building analysis" (Charmaz, 2003). Although there is no quick fix to solve the branding problem of evaluation, an initial step toward that end is for the paradigms and descriptive language used by evaluators to evolve in a way that is appropriately responsive to the changing context in which the field operates.

Context

Futurists can make for frustrating reading—too much hype about technology or fanciful predictions disconnected from reality. This article intends to avoid those extremes by being rooted in the soil of both evaluation theory and practice, describing what seems like an emerging growth out of existing shoots. Therefore, a necessarily brief look back at history sets the context for this look forward.

Although conscious evaluative behavior was arguably a turning point in human evolution, the current professional practice of evaluation dates back to the Great Society projects of the federal government in the early 1960s (Shadish, Cook, & Leviton, 1991). The spirit of that time was expressed in the vision of the "experimenting society" advanced by Campbell, who argued that "the United States and other modern nations should be ready for an experimental approach to social reform, an approach in which we try out new programs designed to cure specific social problems" (Campbell, 1969). These social experiments needed a "process for determining merit, worth or significance" to separate the programs that worked and should be taken to scale from those that did not and should have funding cut (Scriven, 2011). The need for credible determination of what works is the original and still central concern of the field.

Although many evaluations continue within that original paradigm, much has changed in both the field and the broader cultural, political, and economic context. Leaders like Michael Patton blazed a trail toward a broader range of service and value, prompting Scriven to distinguish *evaluators*, those working within the original paradigm, from *evaluation consultants*, for those with broader goals (Scriven, 1997). This distinction was made 1 year before Google was founded and 7 years before Facebook was founded, milestones noted to underscore the scope and pace of cultural and contextual changes since that time.

Vistas of Opportunity

The range of situations that call for an evaluation in the original paradigm is comparably narrow, typically constrained by factors like budget or organizational maturity. The range of situations that call for insightful people both to gather and interpret data in the service of increased effectiveness is vast, and open to a much broader set of budgets and organizational realities. That said, both of these work situations could be accomplished by an evaluator or contracted as part of an evaluation, which seems to misrepresent or limit their full potential.

There seem to be good reasons, including interpersonal connection and associated increase in influence, to define *evaluation* narrowly and reserve its use for those situations that specifically involve judgment of merit, worth, or significance. Not every trip to the doctor involves getting a shot, and deliberately compartmentalizing the threatening part seems worthwhile. Carrying the analogy further, the field of medicine is highly valued (despite the association with fear and pain) because it is the guide and guardian of a universally desired good—physical health. The field of evaluation can also be understood as the guardian and guide of many things, but one in particular stands out as particularly broadly desired—effectiveness.

Toward this end, the original paradigm of evaluation deliberately limited itself to the difficult task of credibly identifying effectiveness, or lack thereof. Indeed, many—though not all—situations require such single-minded focus. The broad-goal approaches to evaluation, which are appropriate for other situations, include the evaluator in more direct contribution toward effectiveness, such as by participating in the intervention itself (i.e., critical theory evaluation) or by helping guide toward greater effectiveness (i.e., formative evaluation, developmental evaluation, etc.). The opportunity for trained, capable professionals to contribute toward increased effectiveness is the vast and growing vista of opportunity about which I am most excited for those gathering under the big tent of evaluation.

The Sensitizing Concept

Though different definitions abound, *effectiveness* is generally understood as the capability of a product or intervention to produce a beneficial impact with at least reasonable efficiency. *Engineering* can be defined as applying knowledge (scientific, mechanical, mathematic, etc.) to the design of anything from the tangible (such as buildings or machines) to the intangible (like a system or process) to meet specific needs. With the building blocks of the term thus outlined, the sensitizing concept, effectiveness engineering, can be defined as *applying the specialized knowledge of the transdiscipline of evaluation to demonstrably improve the beneficial impact and/or efficiency of products, program, or policies.* Thus although Scriven separated *evaluators* from *evaluation consultants*, this approach takes the additional step of dropping the term *evaluation* altogether, with potential benefit for both sides: *Evaluators* are exclusively focused on determinations of merit, worth, or significance, compartmentalizing the threatening connotations of the term *evaluation* to the situations that are in fact potentially threatening. Similarly, the various approaches serving broader goals benefit by shedding a term with threatening connotations and gaining one that emphasizes contribution to the universally desired good of effectiveness.

New Toolbox and Versatile Perspective

Because of the broad range of evaluation approaches that could be associated with the effectiveness engineering paradigm, it is not described by methodology so much as perspective. For example, the practical, problem-solving approach implicit in the word *engineering* implies mixed methods, not either pole of the qualitative/quantitative debate. Furthermore, providing guidance and support within a fast-changing context requires versatility, not specialists or generalists: "Specialists generally have deep skills and narrow scope, giving them expertise that is recognized by peers but seldom valued outside their immediate domain. Generalists have broad scope and shallow skills, enabling them to respond or act reasonably quickly but often without gaining or demonstrating the confidence of their partners or customers.

NEW DIRECTIONS FOR EVALUATION • DOI: 10.1002/ev

Versatilists, in contrast, apply depth of skill to a progressively widening scope of situations and experiences, gaining new competencies, building relationships, and assuming new roles. Versatilists are capable not only of constantly adapting but also of constantly learning and growing" (Friedman, 2007). Effectiveness engineers are thus versatilists within the field of evaluation, willing to learn new methodology and utilize new sources of data. Toward that end, I will conclude with a brief mention of emerging methodology and new data sources that seem especially relevant within the effectiveness engineer frame.

Methodology Related to Systems and Complexity

Although there are many resources on this subject, two new books are specifically geared for evaluators: *Developmental Evaluation: Applying Complexity Concepts to Enhance Innovation and Use* (Patton, 2011) and *Systems Concepts in Action: A Practitioner's Toolkit* (Williams & Hummelbrunner, 2010). These highlight the increasing value of professionals with the training and experience not just to make sense of systems and complexity, but to also provide guidance toward increased effectiveness within those contexts.

Free, Real-Time Data Sources

Google provides two sources of real-time data on actual behavior, in contrast to strictly self-reported behavior like surveys. Google Analytics (Google, 2011a) is a website tracking system that can be embedded into any website, providing a gold mine of data about website visitors and use. Google Insights for Search (Google, 2011b) is a user-friendly interface for Google search traffic data, providing an index of search traffic (not raw traffic totals) for either single search terms or several search terms relative to each other, and the results can be exported as a .csv file for additional analysis. Accurate, relevant, timely data are precious commodities, and Google currently provides vast amounts for free.

Advances in technology and the expanding availability of existing data benefit effectiveness engineers by increasing demand for timely, insightful guidance within the shifting sea of data, and by reducing the cost and time-frame for gathering data.

References

Campbell, D. T. (1969). Reforms as experiments. *American Psychologist, 24,* 409.

Charmaz, K. (2003). Grounded theory: Objectivist and constructivist methods. In N. K. Denzin & Y. S. Lincoln (Eds.), *Strategies for qualitative inquiry* (2nd ed., p. 259). Thousand Oaks, CA: Sage.

Fetterman, D. (2000). *Foundations of empowerment evaluation.* Thousand Oaks, CA: Sage.

Friedman, T. (2007). *The world is flat 3.0: A brief history of the 21st century* (pp. 293–294). New York, NY: Picador.

Google. (2011a). *Google analytics*. Retrieved from http://www.google.com/analytics/
Google. (2011b). *Google insights for search*. Retrieved from http://www.google.com /insights/search/#
Mathison, S. (2005). *Encyclopedia of evaluation* (pp. 92–94, 422). Thousand Oaks, CA: Sage.
Patton, M. Q. (2011). *Developmental evaluation: Applying complexity concepts to enhance innovation and use*. New York, NY: The Guilford Press.
Scriven, M. (1997). Truth and objectivity in evaluation. In E. Chelimsky & W. R. Shadish (Eds.), *Evaluation for the 21st century: A handbook* (pp. 477–500). Thousand Oaks, CA: Sage.
Scriven, M. (2011). *Key evaluation checklist (KEC)* (p. 2). Retrieved from http://michaelscriven.info/images/KEC_1–2.feb2.2011.pdf
Shadish, W. R., Cook, T. D., & Leviton, L. C. (1991). *Foundations of program evaluation: Theories of practice* (pp. 19–28). Newbury Park, CA: Sage.
Williams, B., & Hummelbrunner, R. (2010). *Systems concepts in action: A practitioner's toolkit*. Stanford, CA: Stanford Business Books.

KURT A. WILSON *is a student in the Interdisciplinary PhD in Evaluation program at Western Michigan University and owner of Compass Outreach Media.*

Cohen, D. (2011). Harnessing the power of the electronic health record data for use in program evaluation. In S. Mathison (Ed.), *Really new directions in evaluation: Young evaluators' perspectives. New Directions for Evaluation, 131*, 117–121.

18

Harnessing the Power of the Electronic Health Record Data for Use in Program Evaluation

Deborah Cohen

Abstract

The adoption of the electronic health record (EHR) will play a major role in the evolution of health-related program evaluation and applied research over the next 10 years. As we move toward meeting "meaningful use" standards, many mental health agencies will soon have the capacity to inform internal and external stakeholders about agency processes and outcomes at the click of a mouse. The EHR has become a necessity for business operations among all health-care providers, and it will be important for evaluators to devise ways to utilize this information effectively to guide the program evaluation process. The author describes ways that these data may be used, specifically from the viewpoint of empowerment evaluation, including as a viable secondary data source. © Wiley Periodicals, Inc., and the American Evaluation Association.

Health-record data have always been a potentially rich source of information, even in the days of pure paper records. Health-care providers record and track information on individual client history, diagnostic information, treatment progress, claims data, and financial information. However, any evaluator who has tried to use paper records in order to collect data for a specific study knows that the process is cumbersome and time intensive. As the world changes and as the health-care business is moving toward meeting electronic health record (EHR) meaningful use (Health Information Technology for Economic and Clinical Health Act, [HITECH], 2009), the days of pulling paper charts will end. For evaluators who assess health-care programs it is important to understand what items are being tracked or will be tracked in an agency's EHR and how to access the correct data. This article outlines the basic EHR structure, how the EHR will transform behavioral health organizations, and how EHR data will change access to data for evaluation.

Accessing Data From the Electronic Health Record

The use of health records in research and evaluation is a commonly used approach to collect retrospective information about an individual. In the past, paper records were often incomplete and illegible because of limited quality assurance. Many evaluators do not have the luxury of the time needed to devote to the process. By abstracting data directly from an EHR, data can be directly downloaded into statistical software and only minor recoding is needed before analysis can begin.

To mine the data held in an EHR, it is first important to understand the database. EHRs are primarily relational databases. A relational database stores data in tables (called a relation), which are organized into rows (called a tuple) and columns (called an attribute), based on common characteristics such as client demographics or client service utilization. There are many tables within a complete EHR that contribute to the whole database. Tables in the EHR can be combined to pull together data across tables by matching shared columns in the tables called *unique keys*. A unique key is usually something like the internal client identification number. This means that many of the items within the system are related to one another and can be combined to provide a more complete picture of a particular individual (Beaulieu, 2009).

Depending upon the capacity of the agency in which an evaluator is obtaining data, the agency's IT department may be able to extract whatever data point is selected, but this may not be the case for all of the agencies. In order to obtain data from the system the evaluator may need to know how to mine data from a database. For example, knowledge of SQL, a database computer language designed for managing data in relational database management (Beaulieu, 2009), could be helpful. If an evaluator has experience writing syntax for statistical programs like SAS or SPSS, learning SQL may not be as difficult of an undertaking. Learning to extract data from EHRs may become a necessity for evaluators in the future.

To discover what data elements are available within a specific EHR it is important to learn about what data are being entered. This can be accomplished through observing the workflow of specific providers in an agency. Additionally, one can obtain a database schema from the company that developed the EHR, which lays out visually what tables are in the system and how they are related. It is important to point out that just as there were always missing data elements in paper charts, this has not been fully eliminated through the transition to electronic records. The main difference is that missing data can be discovered through queries, which should save the evaluator time in identifying any potential data problems.

Meaningful Use

A major piece of legislation related to health records was a component of the American Recovery and Reinvestment Act of 2009 (ARRA), the HITECH Act of 2009. The aim of this bill is to motivate providers to adapt EHRs and to improve the nation's health information technology (HIT) infrastructure (Ashish, 2010). The HITECH Act ties dollars to the adoption of a certified EHR within an agency and defines meaningful use through the capacity to complete items such as electronic prescribing, participating in health information exchange, and automated reporting of quality performance. The Act has set lofty goals such as achieving universal EHR use by all health-care providers by 2014 (Ashish, 2010). Why is this piece of legislation important to evaluators? It is important because it may lead to the availability of more complete, readily available data for use in a variety of evaluation studies. The biggest drawback to using secondary data in the past was that every agency collected different information with very little quality assurance to ensure they could provide an evaluator with complete data sets. For many evaluators the biggest concern about using secondary data is reliability and validity of the data. This is why meaningful-use standards will be important to evaluators. As the quality control is increased because of government regulations, health-care data will become a more reliable and valid form of secondary data.

Transforming the Behavioral Health Organization

The strength in EHR implementation is the possibility of all staff members accessing data to improve their daily processes. Many organizations have only had access to data long after the information was collected or through outside parties collecting information for the purpose of an external evaluation. Just because an agency adapts an EHR does not mean anyone will know how to use the data to transform the agency. It is important for evaluators to see the value in teaching agencies how to use their data. Many staff members may be anxious about using data because of a lack of experience or knowledge. Once a staff member realizes that data are accessible to them and comprehends the power of data-informed decision making, he or she will value all forms of evaluation.

This idea of agencywide accountability is in line with the idea of the empowerment evaluation model (Fetterman & Wandersman, 2004). In empowerment evaluation there are 10 principles. In order for an agency to be transformed to use data-informed decision making, 6 of the 10 principles will be very important:

Principle 1: Improvement
Principle 2: Community Ownership
Principle 3: Inclusion
Principle 8: Capacity Building
Principle 9: Organizational Learning
Principle 10: Accountability

The transformation to become a data-driven agency that uses the information from the agency's EHR will take time. The most important step is transforming the agency's culture of organizational learning (Principle 9). The process of feeding back information about how the program is working to all staff, not just administrators, will be the most important value within the organization needed to change the agency's culture. The role of the evaluator is to help the staff learn to interpret the data and put them to good use. This is why Principle 3—inclusion—is important. Many frontline staff have never been given the opportunity to have a say in how their program is working. This points to Principle 2—community ownership. Fetterman and Wandersman (2004) stated that empowerment evaluation necessitates putting evaluation in the hands of program staff. By doing so staff members will have a greater commitment to the findings and use the recommendation.

Once agency staff has buy-in to using data to improve the agency, then Principle 1—improvement, and Principle 10—accountability, can be put into play. The goal is that through working on organizational learning, inclusion, and community ownership, staff members within a program will have a desire to improve their program and be motivated to hold themselves and their group accountable.

Principle 8—capacity building—may look a little different in this situation. Traditionally capacity building refers to teaching program staff and consumers how to conduct their own evaluations by learning about logic models, evaluation design, data collection, analysis, and reporting. Even though all of those elements are very important, the most important element when looking to use the data collected within the EHR is devising a way to access the correct data. When the data collected in the EHR are used for improvement and accountability, the data have already been collected. Just because an agency has an EHR does not mean they have the capacity to extract data from the system. Learning to mine data may be a new role for an evaluator, but obtaining full access to the data already collected is the only way an agency can truly use the whole system to improve the feedback loop of information.

Access to Data in the Future

Many evaluators work for or contract with agencies that are under budgetary constraints (Bamberger, Rugh, & Mabry, 2006), which leads to fewer resources to collect data outside what information is already collected for other purposes. The advantage of using an agency's EHR is that the data have already been collected. However, the information collected internal to an agency may not be sufficient to complete the evaluation (Hatry, 2004). The purpose of this article is not to imply that previous concerns about secondary data have disappeared, but instead to highlight that the new era of electronic records will improve the usability of secondary data. Many of the same barriers to using agency records will still exist but the organization of the data has changed. There will still be missing or incomplete data, changing definitions of data elements, issues linking data from various sources, and privacy concerns (Hatry, 2004). The main difference when working with an EHR versus a paper chart is that some of these items can be discovered much faster, which will leave more time for supplementary data to be collected in a time-limited evaluation.

Evaluators currently have an opportunity to help play a role in improving agency evaluation capacity. If evaluators decide to help in supporting the adaption of EHRs within agencies they will be rewarded later with a greater access to longitudinal data (Penuel & Means, 2011). Just as many evaluators yearn to be included during the program planning process, this will give evaluators an opportunity to develop the database they may use for future studies within the agency. This may be an opportunity to support an agency to use data in a meaningful way, and in turn increase staff buy-in to evaluation in general.

References

American Recovery and Reinvestment Act of 2009, Title IV—Health Information Technology for Economic and Clinical Act, 111th Cong., 1st Sess. (2009).

Ashish, J. K. (2010). Meaningful use of electronic health records: The road ahead. *Journal of American Medical Association, 304*(15), 1709–1710.

Bamberger, M., Rugh, J., & Mabry, L. (2006). *Realworld evaluation: Working under budget, time, data and political constraints.* Thousand Oaks, CA: Sage.

Beaulieu, A. (2009). *Learning SQL* (2nd ed.). Sebastapol, CA: O'Reilly.

Fetterman, D. M., & Wandersman, A. (2004). *Empowerment evaluation principles in practice.* New York, NY: Guilford Press.

Hatry, H. P. (2004). Using agency records. In J. S. Wholey, H. P. Hatry, & K. E. Newcomer (Eds.), *Handbook of practical program evaluation* (2nd ed., pp. 396–412). San Francisco, CA: Jossey-Bass.

Penuel, W. R., & Means, B. (2011). Using large scale databases in evaluation: Advances, opportunities, and challenges. *American Journal of Evaluation, 32,*118–133.

DEBORAH COHEN *is the director of evaluation for Community Mental Health Center, Inc., overseeing the internal program evaluation of a rural mental health center in southeastern Indiana.*

Galen, M., & Grodzicki, D. (2011). Utilizing emerging technology in program evaluation. In S. Mathison (Ed.), *Really new directions in evaluation: Young evaluators' perspectives. New Directions for Evaluation, 131*, 123–128.

19

Utilizing Emerging Technology in Program Evaluation

Matthew Galen, Deborah Grodzicki

Abstract

The force of fast-paced technological growth and globalization influence today's organizational environments. Successful organizations have become more nimble and responsive to these environmental realities, while simultaneously managing increasingly complex informational needs. The success of program evaluations will depend on evaluators' abilities to leverage future technologies to produce and disseminate knowledge in an accessible and actionable form. The authors propose that the roles and responsibilities of the evaluator will shift as current evaluation approaches are adapted to make effective use of these technological tools. Specifically, the authors discuss evaluators' future roles as collaborators with design-science practitioners, filterers and translators of information, and customizers of knowledge dissemination. © Wiley Periodicals, Inc., and the American Evaluation Association.

Evaluators are uniquely poised to help organizations cope with an increasingly uncertain and complex world. We consider a variety of technological innovations in the context of globalization trends to understand their implications for the future of program evaluation. Those better able to understand, anticipate, and influence these trends will have greater capacity to exert a positive impact on organizations. We assert that evaluators must constantly scan for emerging technologies, consider their

NEW DIRECTIONS FOR EVALUATION, no. 131, Fall 2011 © Wiley Periodicals, Inc., and the American Evaluation Association. Published online in Wiley Online Library (wileyonlinelibrary.com) • DOI: 10.1002/ev.389

utility, and selectively deploy them in practice. As a discipline, we must respond to technological shifts and the forces of globalization by expanding our concepts of evaluators' roles and responsibilities for producing and disseminating organizational knowledge. We will discuss how emerging technological innovations may be leveraged to facilitate organizational learning and evaluation utilization.

Knowledge Production

The rapid evolution of online applications has altered our ideas about what it means to produce knowledge. Flexible, open systems such as Twitter and Facebook have reshaped our world in ways we are only just beginning to understand. They empower groups of users to interact in mundane and unexpected ways, from connecting with old friends to fomenting revolution in the Middle East. A useful by-product for systems such as these is information about users' behaviors. As evaluators in organizations, we can learn from these examples by developing and utilizing flexible knowledge management systems (KMSs) that gather data from people and the environment, automatically converting it into structured information. We anticipate that evaluators will increasingly collaborate in the development of KMSs, guide their management, and translate the resulting data, with the ultimate purpose of informing decision making.

The definition of KMSs varies in the literature, but we find the definition offered by Alavi and Leidner (2001) the most comprehensive: "Knowledge Management Systems refer to a class of information systems applied to managing organizational knowledge. That is, they are [information technology]-based systems developed to support and enhance the organizational processes of knowledge creation, storage/retrieval, transfer, and application" (p. 114). Within this definition, KMSs can take multiple forms, from simple message boards to opportunities for people to connect using a variety of interfaces and databases.

Wikipedia is an example of a large-scale knowledge management system. At a high level, users contribute textual data to Wikipedia, which stores the data as information on the website, from which other users can access and modify it. Although Wikipedia is an easily recognizable example, diverse KMSs are ubiquitous. When applied to the organizational context, it is easy to understand practitioners' excitement about the potential for powerful KMSs to enable organizations to respond quickly to varying environmental conditions, endowing them with the strategic flexibility needed in rapidly changing, complex environments (Stata, 1989).

Information systems (IS) professionals predict that emerging technological innovations combined with a rapid pace of environmental change will increase demand for and use of these systems within organizations (Smuts, Merwe, Loock, & Kotzé, 2009). To respond to this future demand, evaluators can collaborate with practitioners working within the design-science paradigm. The design-science paradigm grew out of the intellectual tradition of engineering, whereas theoretical prescriptions for evaluation practice are typically derived from the social sciences. Design science, therefore, focuses on problem solving and the development of technological innovations (Simon, 1996). In contrast, evaluation typically applies derivatives of the iterative theory-building approach in general social science toward program assessment. Recent discussions of evaluation capacity building, however, have highlighted the evaluator's role in working with the organizational systems and structures that enable sustainable learning and knowledge production (Preskill & Boyle, 2008). We envision an expanded role of the evaluator as a collaborator with design-science professionals in the development of these knowledge management structures.

Successfully developing KMSs to build evaluation capacity requires that system processes not only fulfill the technical requirements of data storage and retrieval, but also accommodate the organization's culture, values, policies, and procedures (Smuts et al., 2009). The complicated nature of such a project necessitates interdisciplinary collaboration between professionals with skill sets in evaluation, IS, and information technology (IT). Evaluators can enhance the development of KMS processes by determining organizations' knowledge strengths and knowledge needs to align KMSs with organizational processes. Evaluators can also assist in updating these processes by continually monitoring KMSs and ensuring that they are responsive to changing organizational and environmental needs.

Without thoughtful human interpretation, KMSs, however useful, merely manage flows of information and data. In addition to collaborating with IS and IT professionals in the development and management of KMSs, evaluators of the future can enhance the knowledge-production capabilities of KMSs by filtering and translating the information these systems produce. The constant information flow produced by these systems may be useful to stakeholders making relatively straightforward decisions. When approaching complex problems with many interconnected components, however, evaluators can facilitate decision making by converting KMS information output into actionable knowledge. Evaluators may highlight pertinent information and present it as a coherent narrative that is accessible to relevant stakeholders.

The increasing sophistication of KMSs and concurrent rise in demand will have implications for the evaluation practitioners of the future. When properly designed, these systems may provide critical support for evaluative processes and help to promote evidence-based thinking within and between organizations. Given the potential utility of these systems to enhance evaluations and promote organizational learning, practicing evaluators should consider incorporating KMS development and management into their repertoire of skills and service offerings. Evaluator-optimized systems can then serve as repositories of organizational knowledge, and should simplify the logistics of designing and implementing evaluations.

Knowledge Dissemination

To meet the demands of increasingly globalized and diverse organizational environments, evaluation practitioners can make use of emerging technological innovations that enable high-impact transfer of evaluation findings (Chouinard & Cousins, 2009). We anticipate substantial development in these knowledge-transfer methods during the next decade, allowing evaluators to disseminate streams of information globally, customized to the individual needs and preferences of their audiences. These tools will not automatically endow evaluators with cultural competence, but will serve to enhance evaluators' existing skill sets.

Current Web applications use customized content to suit users' needs and preferences. The popular Web-based media rental site, Netflix, for instance, gathers data about users' habits and reviews, as well as the habits and reviews of their friends, so that it may present users with recommended media most likely to meet their approval. Customized outputs such as Netflix's highlight the information that is most relevant for a given user. Many evaluators already use a similar approach to disseminating findings; they develop separate reports and customize presentations to meet a selected group's needs. Netflix-style content customization, however, can capture users' tacit information needs and draw from large databases in order to "recommend" films that users would not have discovered on their own. By creatively incorporating similar user-customized information outputs into practice, evaluators will be able to tailor information dissemination to the level of the group or individual.

Cutting-edge methods for promoting knowledge dissemination may go one step further, tailoring not only *which* information is disseminated to users, but also *how* it is disseminated. The work of information design luminary Edward Tufte, in particular, has raised the profile of visual displays to the level of art–science hybrid. Sparklines is one such visual technique developed by Tufte, used for communicating large amounts of data in a compact, visually pleasing, and easy-to-understand format. Visual display methods such as Sparklines draw from cognitive principles to minimize viewers' information-processing burden and eliminate barriers to understanding (Tufte, 2001). We can learn an important lesson from the masters of information design: The format of information matters. In fact, the information and the format are inextricably intertwined. In order for information to have the best chance of becoming knowledge, it must be visually rich yet easily accessed and understood. Through the use of these methods, evaluators can enhance their audiences' understanding of evaluation findings, ultimately increasing their utility.

The continuation of this trend toward greater information customization is the combination and extension of content customization and form customization. Emerging innovations will tailor *which* information is shown and *how* it is shown, taking *individual differences* into account. In the globalized organizational contexts of the future, evaluation audiences will be increasingly culturally diverse, utilizing varied cognitive and learning styles. As a simple example, an English-reading program manager who reads from left to right may tend to focus her attention on the top-left portion of a display, whereas a Hebrew-reading program manager who reads from right to left may focus on the top-right portion of a display. These culturally influenced cognitive styles underscore the importance of customizing visual displays to accommodate diverse audiences. Furthermore, matching information content and form to the audiences' cognitive styles may result in greater learning (Hawk & Shah, 2007). Evaluators have the responsibility, therefore, to respond and adapt to the cognitive styles and cultural perspectives of their audiences. Emerging technologies will provide evaluators with tools necessary to meet this growing need for differentiated communication.

Discussion

In this article, we have looked at some ways in which technology will expand the existing roles and responsibilities of evaluators as knowledge producers and knowledge disseminators. Evaluators can look forward to facilitating sustainable organizational knowledge production by collaborating on the development and management of KMS infrastructures with design-science professionals in the IS and IT fields. These systems should soon be ubiquitous, and the torrential information flows that they produce may threaten to overwhelm stakeholders' information-processing capabilities. Evaluators can serve as organizational guides by filtering these flows from KMSs and converting them into meaningful and accessible knowledge.

As knowledge disseminators, evaluators will have greater responsibilities as customizers of information to the needs of their audiences. These needs and preferences will be increasingly diverse, but new technological innovations may help evaluators meet this challenge, facilitating audience learning by automatically tailoring information content and form to groups and individuals. The potential utility of these tools warrants evaluator attention. By developing an intimate understanding of emerging knowledge dissemination technology, evaluators can purposefully integrate them into evaluation practice.

The evaluators that currently incorporate these technologies into their practices are practitioners Rogers (1962) might term "early adopters" or even "innovators" within the discipline. Although KMSs and user-customized information outputs have been around for several years, their diffusion among practitioners is still at a nascent stage. At their current stage of diffusion, these innovations are optional and moderately useful tools used by enterprising evaluators. If these technologies follow the relatively predictable patterns of successful innovations, however, then in the near future they will likely be adopted by a critical mass of users in evaluation and other disciplines. The impact of these technologies will rapidly increase as an

NEW DIRECTIONS FOR EVALUATION • DOI: 10.1002/ev

expanding community of evaluators and stakeholders use them to communicate with one another. It is at this point that these innovations will truly begin to reshape the roles and responsibilities of evaluators.

As technological innovations rapidly evolve, we must anticipate their impact on the discipline of evaluation and adapt our roles judiciously. As evaluators, we are optimistic about the creative information-engagement facilitated by recent technology. We must be thoughtful in our adoption of these innovations, though, lest we risk evaluators losing the human touch that distinguishes our contributions to organizational cultures. We must engage with technology and anticipate its impact, not only as a means of enhancing our service to society, but also to ensure that we do not lose our core values, principles, and convictions.

References

Alavi, M., & Leider, D. (2001). Review: Knowledge management and knowledge management systems: Conceptual foundations and research issues. *MIS Quarterly, 25*(1), 107–136.

Chouinard, J. A., & Cousins, J. B. (2009). A review and synthesis of current research on cross-cultural evaluation. *American Journal of Evaluation, 30*(4), 457–494.

Hawk, T. F., & Shah, A. J. (2007). Using learning style instruments to enhance student learning. *Decision Sciences Journal of Innovative Education, 5*(1), 1–19.

Preskill, H., & Boyle, S. (2008). A multidisciplinary model of evaluation capacity building. *American Journal of Evaluation, 29*(4), 443–459.

Rogers, E. M. (1962). *Diffusion of innovations.* New York, NY: The Free Press.

Simon, H. A. (1996). *The sciences of the artificial.* Boston, MA: MIT Press.

Smuts, H., Merwe, A.V.D., Loock, M., & Kotzé, P. (2009, October). A framework and methodology for knowledge management system implementation. In *Proceedings of the 2009 Annual Research Conference of the South African Institute of Computer Scientists and Information Technologists—SAICSIT '09* (pp. 70–79). New York, NY: ACM Press.

Stata, R. (1989). Organizational learning: The key to management innovation. *Sloan Management Review, 30*, 63–74.

Tufte, E. R. (2001). *The visual display of quantitative information* (2nd ed.). Cheshire, CT: Graphics Press.

MATTHEW GALEN *is a doctoral student in the School of Behavioral and Organizational Sciences at Claremont Graduate University.*

DEBORAH GRODZICKI *is a doctoral student in the Department of Social Research Methodology at the University of California, Los Angeles.*

20

Online Learning Programs: Evaluation's Challenging Future

Derek Nord

Abstract

With the vast array of contextual factors, pedagogical approaches, models of implementation, and purposes of education and training related to online learning, educators, learners, and the general public alike are seeking answers regarding utility and effectiveness of online learning. This article identifies and responds to many of the challenges and issues related to the evaluation of online learning that will likely test evaluators in the years and decades to come. The author provides an early conceptualization of a comprehensive evaluation framework to focus evaluation on the many components of online learning rather than a narrow aspect. © Wiley Periodicals, Inc., and the American Evaluation Association.

O ver the last decade, distance education and training expanded well beyond the once-innovative television and audio- and videocassette. As technology continues its advancement, so too does the evolving world of learning. Today, there is a deluge of educational and training mechanisms that exploit the power and scope of the internet (Moore & Kearsley, 1996). Like its technological cousins, online learning can more efficiently reach a wider audience than traditional face-to-face methods. So long as a learner has access to an internet connection, he or she can receive education and training anytime and anywhere, thus expanding the reach, scope, and accessibility of education, as well as learning resources (Rosenberg, 2001).

On the surface, online learning is an easy concept to understand for a public that is technologically savvy. It is merely the delivery of instruction through a device that delivers the instructional material via an internet connection. However, this concept is far more difficult to grasp when one considers the diversity of approaches and uses of online learning in all sectors of our society. This instructional mechanism can take on a limited or expansive role in the educational process. It can provide information much like a book provides information to a student. It can provide sequenced instruction and assessment much like a teacher provides instruction. Learning can be enhanced with audio and video, practice exercises, and a number of other learning strategies. Adding another dimension of complexity to online training is the role of the human educator or trainer in facilitating learning. For some, the online information and instruction supplants human instruction and interaction, whereas others see the role of the educator as the primary instructor and online delivery as supporting materials (Ginsburg, 1998). The advancements in online learning have grown to encompass many different designs and variations, some of which include online learning communities (Russell & Ginsburg, 2000), microeducation (Hug, 2005), blended human–computer-delivered education (Garrison & Vaughan, 2007), virtual school (U.S. Department of Education, 2008), and asynchronous instruction (Berge, 1999).

With relatively modest costs and an exceptionally efficient delivery mechanism, the demand for online educational and training has exploded in recent years. Yet the field of online learning continues to be relatively slow to adopt the informative, developmental, and at times critical attention of program evaluation, despite a growing acceptance of the benefit of evaluation at all levels. This is because of the many technical and methodological barriers evaluators of online programs often encounter when learners are using new technology in multiple settings (U.S. Department of Education, 2008). Despite these challenges and many more, evaluation's future is one directly linked to the expansive field of online learning.

Adding to this challenge, for evaluators, is the limited work that has been done to create an evaluation framework that identifies and agrees on rules and prohibitions for evaluating these educational programs (Alkin, 2004). As a result, it is difficult for evaluators working in these settings to have a clear picture about the areas that need evaluative attention and appropriate approaches to use in understanding them. The development of a comprehensive and guiding framework to understand and approach the evaluation of online learning can act as a foundation from which evaluators can focus their efforts. The following section provides the early conceptualization of such a framework by positing the major aspects needing evaluative attention. Because of the limited research on this topic and the complexity of online learning, it is important to recognize that this early framework requires considerable theoretical and practical development and testing. Regardless, this framework can act as a point from which to begin. The key components to this framework include the online learning program, utilization, implementation context, and outcomes.

What Is an Online Learning Program?

A common and immediate challenge for evaluators approaching online learning is defining the evaluand, or online learning program being evaluated. This is likely due to two key factors. First, the diversity and scalability of online learning programs make it difficult to compare programs reliably. Secondly, the virtual and distance nature of many aspects of online learning makes it difficult to understand the learner–instruction interface or the learning process. Unlike face-to-face instruction, there is often limited or no human assurance or oversight to ensure learners engage and experience the instruction at a minimal level. As a result, evaluators are likely to encounter an educational black box, where they are able to assess specific outcomes but are challenged to evaluate the process of achieving these outcomes. Only after evaluators understand the unique breadth of online programs and have deep knowledge of the instructional mechanism occurring in the program they are evaluating can they develop proper questions and methods to respond.

A common theme across all online learning programs is the presentation of educational or training content. This may be delivered with a wide range and combination of media, such as text, narration, audio, and video. Content may be prepackaged and sold by a training company, developed by an individual educator, or created by a business to train its workforce, or it might link to existing Web resources.

Considerable variation in instructional models exists across programs to support online learning. Programs tend to fall on a spectrum where some use purely technologically delivered strategies and others merge the skills of human educators with that of the online program. In addition, supporting activities are often used by way of virtual or real-life delivery to enhance and reinforce one's learning. For example, this may include practice opportunities, reflection exercises, and homework assignments.

Online programs incorporate an assessment process that seeks to understand whether learners acquired the knowledge, skill, or attitudes presented and taught through the educational content and instruction. An often-used approach is that of online testing, usually implemented with the use of multiple-choice items. Not only are these typically easier to develop, they are also easier for current technology to score. Because of the limitations of simple testing to assess changes in one's skills, many online programs also incorporate a number of more advanced assessment procedures, such as portfolio assessment and on-the-job demonstration.

Implementation Context

The experiences and outcomes of learners and organizations employing on-line learning programs are often driven at the local level. When there is alignment in individual and organizational needs of education and training, implementation is often a smoother process. However, when individual development needs differ from the organizational needs, a tension between the learner and organization can develop and affect the implementation of program activities. This can result in a hindering of the educational process and require organizational exertion of control to facilitate the activities (Knowles, Holton, & Swanson, 2005). Thus, organizations, regardless of the type, have a major role to play in implementing online learning programs. Organizational leaders often play a large role in rolling out, implementing, and ensuring ongoing use of an online training program include changing learning behavioral patterns, providing a vision for expected performance changes, and motivating learners (Allen, 2003).

Organizations also require a level of technological, managerial, supervisory, and cultural readiness across the various sites the program will touch. Organizational models of implementation are emerging to support and facilitate more effective use of online programs by providing guidance to organizations to align learning to meet the needs of the learner and the organization, and define processes, infrastructure, roles, and skills needed to execute programs. To ensure their effectiveness, current and future models of implementation require evaluative attention. In addition, comprehensive evaluation of online programs must account for these structural and systemic nuances from which a program is being realized.

Utilization

Data about online education programs can be vast, depending on the program and the type of data-collection system in place. It also allows for an assessment of program performance against its intended use. Rossi, Freeman, and Lipsey (1999) point out that monitoring data, such as who uses the program and how they use the program, provides for more than a single opportunity for evaluation and research; rather, it allows for a variety of approaches and methods that can be used to answer many evaluation questions. Utilization data can allow for assessment and judgment of program components by investigating a number of areas, such as the population using the program, the extent of program use, what components are being accessed, and when and how learners are engaging online learning.

As evaluators seek to assess various components of online learning programs, they will encounter different concepts of program users depending on the level they approach their work. Microlevel evaluation is likely to focus on the learner who is engaging the program. However, many evaluations also seek to understand program use at a higher level, such as schools, businesses, and even states. Such a perspective requires evaluators to assume a broad definition of *user* within and between each evaluation.

An important design feature for many online programs is its ability to capture and store utilization data. This may include information about when and what materials were accessed, how much material was accessed, and the extent learning was completed. For evaluators, this is an important step to monitoring key aspects of program delivery.

Outcomes

Ultimately, online programs seek to produce positive outcomes for their users; at the microlevel users include individual learners, and at the meso- and macrolevels users may include school districts and schools, businesses and related sites, states, or other defined users utilizing the approach. Identifying and prioritizing outcomes across these user groups is a challenge for evaluators, because no known or agreed-upon outcome measures or indicators exist in the evaluation or online learning fields. Until such guidance exists, evaluators must minimally rely on the program's intended purpose as guidance at each of these user levels. Microlevel outcomes likely, at minimum, relate to learning, such as changes in knowledge, skills, and attitudes. The broader, higher-level outcomes can be more difficult to pinpoint, because education and training are most often viewed and understood as an individual intervention rather than one implemented at a higher level. In reality, online programs are often charged with achieving meso- and macrolevel outcomes. At these higher levels, outcomes are often more linked to the context in which online learning was sought by an organization in the first place, such as improving organizational performance and efficiency, providing a more cost-effective or efficient educational approach, expanding reach of and access to learning, or reducing workforce challenges related to training.

At times the intended outcomes for the individual learner and at the higher levels will be in alignment. However, this is not always the case. Evaluators will encounter programs where an intended outcome at one level negatively affects the outcomes at another level. For example, an organization's goal to provide a more cost-efficient online program may result in the elimination of on-the-job demonstration and human critique, thus limiting individual skill acquisition. When approaching online programs it is important for evaluators to avoid ignoring these different perspectives on outcomes. By addressing one level over another, evaluators risk overlooking key program features, which can lead to misleading findings and irrelevant recommendations. Evaluators working in online learning environments will require this broad and multifaceted understanding of the programs they assess. They must be able to move between these different levels, and must also have the skills to merge what they learn from each level to understand the online program in a comprehensive manner.

Conclusion

Moving forward, there is a need for open discussion and debate regarding the use and effectiveness of online learning programs. Evaluation can play a fundamental role in guiding and informing this attention. This initial framework provides the beginnings of a structure to understand the key aspects that evaluators of online programs must understand and where to focus their professional attention. Formative or summative, narrow or comprehensive in scope, the future of evaluation will be directly linked to online learning programs as investments continue to be made in the learning approach. Evaluators must take the torch and perform the considerable work needed to expand on a framework not only to understand evaluative aspects of online learning as presented here, but also to advance methodological and theoretical approaches to understand and evaluate online programs.

References

Alkin, M. (Ed.). (2004). *Evaluation roots: Tracing theorists' views and influences.* Thousand Oaks, CA: Sage.

Allen, M. (2003). *Michael Allen's guide to e-learning: Building interactive, fun, and effective learning programs for any company.* Hoboken, NJ: John Wiley & Sons.

Berge, Z. (1999). Interaction in post-secondary Web-based learning. *Educational Technology, 39*(1), 5–11.

Garrison, R., & Vaughan, N. (2007). *Blended learning in higher education: Framework, principles, and guidelines.* Hoboken, NJ: Jossey-Bass.

Ginsburg, L. (1998). Integrating technology into adult learning. In C. E. Hopey (Ed.), *Technology, basic skills, and adult education: Getting ready and moving forward* (pp. 37–45). Columbus, OH: Center on Education and Training for Employment.

Hug, T. (2005). *Exploring possibilities of utilization of narrations and storytelling for the designing of "micro units" and didactical micro-learning arrangements.* Paper presented at the fourth Media in Transition conference. Cambridge, MA: MIT.

Knowles, M., Holton, E., & Swanson, R. (2005). *The adult learner: The definitive classic in adult education and human resource development.* New York, NY: Elsevier.

Moore, M., & Kearsley, G. (1996). *Distance education: A systems view.* Boston, MA: Wadsworth.

Rosenberg, M. (2001). *E-learning: Strategies for delivering knowledge in the digital age.* New York, NY: McGraw-Hill.

Rossi, P., Freeman, H., & Lipsey, M. (1999). *Evaluation: A systematic approach.* Thousand Oaks, CA: Sage.

Russell, M., & Ginsburg, L. (2000). *Learning online: Extending the meaning of community. A review of three programs from the Southeastern United States.* Philadelphia, PA: National Center for Adult Literacy.

U.S. Department of Education. (2008). *Evaluating online learning: Challenges and strategies for success.* Washington, DC: Office of Innovation and Improvement.

DEREK NORD *is a research associate in the Institute on Community Integration's Research and Training Center on Community Living and Employment at the University of Minnesota.*

INDEX

A

Accountability: empowerment evaluation model in line with, 119–120; push for organizational, 77

AEA365 A Tip-a-Day by and for Evaluators, 68

African American community family health program, 8, 11

Ahmed, S. M., 60, 61, 62, 63

Al-Talal, B. B., 99

Alavi, M., 124

Alkin, M. C., 53, 69, 130

Allen, J., 36

Allen, M., 132

American Evaluation Association (AEA): Feminist Issues topical interest group of, 53, 57; Thought Leader's Forum of, 83, 87; 25th anniversary of the, 1–4

American Recovery and Reinvestment Act (ARRA), 119

Anand, V., 98, 99, 100

Anderson, S., 1

Angermeier, L., 8

AoL (America Online), 48

Aotearoa New Zealand: description of, 72; evaluation of Pākehā (non-Māori) and Māori societies in, 72–75

Aotearoa New Zealand evaluators: board influences on direction of craft, 72–73; emerging directions of two different, 72; importance of brokering relationships in evaluation, 73–75; social navigation approach of, 75

Argyris, C., 22

Ashish, J. K., 119

Automatic memory, 98

B

Baker, E., 61

Baldwin, K., 35, 36

Bamberger, M., 107, 121

Barbour, R. S., 48

Baxter, C. E., 4, 77, 81

Beaulieu, A., 118

Beck, B., 60

Behavioral health organizations: EHR (electric health record) used in evaluations of, 117–121; empowerment evaluation principles for, 119–120

Berge, Z., 130

Bheda, D., 4, 53, 58

Birkland, T., 94

Blagg, R. D., 4, 27, 30

Blalock, A. B., 104, 106

Boulton, A., 4, 71, 76

Boyle, S., 125

Branding evaluation, 111–112

Braveman, P., 59

Brisolara, S., 53

"But Is It Rigorous? Trustworthiness and Authenticity in Naturalistic Evaluation" (Guba & Lincoln), 2

C

Campbell, D. T., 24, 31, 32, 33, 113

Campbell, M. K., 48

Carael, M., 92

Carman, J., 94

Centers for Disease Control and Prevention (CDC), 60

Charmaz, K., 112

Chavajay, P., 12

Chelimsky, E., 78

Chen, H. T., 28

Chouinard, J. A., 126

Christian, L. M., 44

Christie, C. A., 33, 53, 69

Chun, M. M., 43

Cincinnati directory assessment: charges for, 34; effects of response costs in charging for, 35*fig*

Cleveland, W. S., 43, 44

Cockburn, L., 63

Coffee Break webinars, 68

Coffman, J., 16

Cohen, D., 4, 117, 121

Collective memory, 98

Collins, P. H., 54

Common Rule, 49

Community: evaluator development of resources within the, 63; knowledge of the, 62–63; relationships between evaluators and leaders of, 61–62

Community Stress Prevention Center (CSPC) [Israel], 48–49

Community-based evaluation (CBPR): challenges and solutions for evaluators, 61–62; description of, 60–61; knowledge of the community importance to, 62–63; relationships with community leaders during, 61–62; resources required for, 63

Condom use education campaign, 35–36, 37*fig*

Confidentiality issues, 49–50. *See also* Ethical issues

Connell, N.A.D., 98

Conner, R., 74

Conscious memory, 98

Cook, T. D., 31, 32, 33, 113

Corbett, J. M., 98

Coryn, C.L.S., 4, 31, 32, 33, 39

Cousins, C. B., 2

Cousins, J. B., 126

Cowan, N., 43

Craik, F.I.M., 43

Cram, F., 73

Crane, S., 66

Critique of Pure Reason (Kant), 22

Cronbach's UTOS (units, treatment, observations, settings), 83–84

Croninger, R., 23

Cultural competence: avoiding stereotypes in efforts to bolster, 11–12; connecting evaluation to ST for, 9*t*–10*t*